Hacked and Hunted: A Smart Girl's Guide to Online Safety

Anand Shinde and Vandana Keswani

Published by DevOM Publishing, 2025.

Table of Contents

Dedication

"This book is dedicated to every girl or woman, especially to my wonderful daughter, Aarushi Shinde, who is navigating the ever-evolving digital landscape and facing its challenges with courage and resilience. It is also a tribute to those tirelessly working to make our online world safer for all. May your journey through the digital world be secure, informed, and empowered."

With Gratitude,

Vandana Keswani & Anand Shinde

Published by DevOM Publishing 2025

ISBN 978-1-916865-27-3

Acknowledgements

"I want to begin by expressing my deepest gratitude to my incredible wife, Shilpa Shinde, and my wonderful daughter, Aarushi Shinde. It's hard to find words that truly capture how much your love, understanding, and unwavering belief in me have meant. Your constant emotional support, patience, and the countless sacrifices you both made throughout this journey have been my strength. Without you, this book would not have been possible. I am beyond fortunate to walk through life with you by my side.

I am incredibly grateful to my spiritual mentor, Shri Rahul Makhi Guruji, who has been guiding me on my spiritual journey. He is responsible for my spiritual, personal, and professional growth. Without his selfless and honest guidance, my progress would never have been possible.

I want to extend my deepest gratitude to Dhanya Menon, India's first female cybercrime investigator, whose relentless efforts in tackling cyber threats have been instrumental in raising awareness about online safety. Through Avanzo Cyber Security Solutions, she has empowered countless individuals-especially women-to take control of their digital presence. My sincere appreciation also goes to Dr. Debarati Halder, a leading cyber law expert and tireless advocate for victims of online abuse. As the co-founder and Managing Director of the Centre for Cyber Victim Counselling (CCVC), her groundbreaking research has bridged critical gaps in India's cyber laws, ensuring better protection for victims of digital violence. I am also profoundly grateful to Kriti Sharma, a prominent advocate for digital safety and privacy, whose tireless work in cybersecurity education and awareness has encouraged women to take control of their online security and played a significant role in shaping the message of this book.

A special acknowledgement goes to Dr. Jessica Barker, a leading voice in cybersecurity, whose efforts to educate the public, particularly women, about the risks of cybercrime and online harassment have been invaluable. Her work has inspired greater digital awareness and provided individuals with the tools to protect themselves. Lastly, my sincere gratitude to Eva Galperin, Director of Cybersecurity at the Electronic Frontier Foundation (EFF), whose advocacy in fighting cyberstalking and improving data security has made a lasting impact on online safety, particularly for women navigating digital spaces.

To all these incredible women-your dedication to making the digital world safer inspires me daily. This book is a small contribution to the ongoing fight for cybersecurity awareness and a tribute to the vital work you do."

Foreword

Mannu Chaudhary,

In today's hyperconnected world, the line between the real and the virtual is fading fast. The internet, once celebrated as the most significant enabler of human connection, has also become a breeding ground for deception, manipulation, and exploitation. It offers the promise of limitless opportunity and yet, behind every click lurks the potential for loss. Hacked and Hunted: A Smart Girl's Guide to Online Safety captures this tension masterfully, transforming the abstract idea of "cyber danger" into a profoundly human story of trust, betrayal, and resilience.

The book brings to life three young women - Aarushi, Kaneera, and Sophia - whose journeys mirror the experiences of millions navigating the digital world today. Through their story, we see how a moment of joy online can spiral into a nightmare of cyberstalking, data theft, and shattered privacy. Yet, what makes this book remarkable is not just its realism, but its purpose. Beneath the thrilling narrative lies an urgent message: awareness is the first line of defense, and knowledge is the greatest weapon against digital predators.

Authors Anand Shinde and Vandana Keswani, both seasoned cybersecurity professionals, have crafted more than a novel - they've created a mirror for our times. They show how empowerment begins with understanding the risks and reclaiming control over one's digital life. The book not only entertains but educates - teaching readers how to recognize online threats, protect their personal information, and stand firm in the face of cyber adversity.

In many ways, Hacked and Hunted reflects our shared digital reality. It warns, guides, and empowers - reminding us that while technology evolves, human vigilance remains timeless. As we journey with Aarushi, Kaneera, and Sophia through their trials, we are reminded of a simple truth: safety in the digital age is not a privilege, but a responsibility.

This book is a must-read for every parent, teacher, and young reader who lives, learns, and dreams online. It's not just a story about being hacked - it's a story about fighting back.

Preface

"The online world is a dangerous game of risks and rewards. It promises connection, opportunity, and convenience, but it also harbors unseen dangers-lurking in the shadows, waiting for the slightest mistake. "Hacked and Hunted: A Girl's Journey to Online Safety" pulls you into a heart-pounding race against time where every click, every post, every interaction is fraught with peril.

Aarushi, Kaneera, and Sophia are three friends bound by their unique strengths. Aarushi, a tech genius, thrives in the world of zeros and ones, always one step ahead in the battle against online threats. Kaneera, a fast-rising social media star, basks in the glow of her online fame, blissfully unaware of the dark side of her success. And Sophia, a law student with a relentless drive for justice, begins to uncover the true cost of living in the digital age. Their lives are forever changed when a celebration of Kaneera's social media milestone quickly turns into a nightmare.

What starts as innocent fun-photos, hashtags, and followers-soon spirals into a terrifying game of cat and mouse. A hacker's malicious hand reaches out, targeting their every move, using phishing scams, cyberstalking, and data theft to tear their world apart. From spyware crawling through their devices to personal data being sold on the dark web, the three women are drawn into a web of digital deception that seems impossible to escape.

With every twist, every revelation, the stakes grow higher, and the consequences more deadly. Kaneera's fame becomes a weapon against her. Aarushi's tech skills are put to the ultimate test as she digs deeper into the hacker's world, only to find that the line between the predator and the prey is blurring. And Sophia, fighting to protect her friends, realizes that the threat is not just from the outside-but from within.

This is not just a thriller; it's a wake-up call. A story of survival in a world where privacy is a lie and trust can be shattered with a single keystroke. As Aarushi, Kaneera, and Sophia fight to reclaim their lives, the reader will be left on the edge of their seat, racing to uncover the truth before it's too late.

"Hacked and Hunted" will make you rethink every password, every post, and every click. Because in this world, nothing is ever as safe as it seems."

About the Author

"ANAND SHINDE IS A RENOWNED, seasoned Cybersecurity expert, mentor, and author with a wealth of experience in safeguarding digital ecosystems, as a certified professional with credentials from global leaders like Microsoft, Cisco, Amazon, ISACA and the International Society of Automation. Anand has worked on complex cybersecurity projects across India, Poland, Ireland, and the United States. His international career has equipped him with diverse perspectives and practical insights to address intricate cybersecurity challenges effectively.

In addition to his consulting work, Anand is deeply committed to education and mentorship. Since 2015, he has been serving as a student mentor and career counsellor for prestigious institutions, including Novel Group of Institutes and MIT ADT University, guiding aspiring professionals toward successful careers in cybersecurity. His role as a mentor for the International Society of Automation reflects his dedication to fostering talent in the ever-evolving cyber landscape.

Anand has also contributed to the field of cybersecurity and artificial intelligence with an innovative patent application, underscoring his commitment to advancing the industry. His contributions extend to raising cyber awareness through blogs and campaigns that promote best practices for digital strength.

For anyone aspiring to build a career in cybersecurity, Anand invites you to connect through AnandShinde.com, where he continues to empower individuals and organizations to thrive in the digital age."

About the Author

"WITH OVER 18 YEARS of hands-on experience in cyber defense, Vandana Keswani brings a rare blend of technical depth, leadership acumen, and human perspective to this book. As an Operations Manager (Enterprise Cyber Security) at Fujitsu, Vandana has spent her career safeguarding organizations across India, the UK, and the Netherlands-working in diverse sectors such as banking, fashion, sports apparel, and food & beverages.

Armed with a Master's degree and executive specialization in IT & Management from Welingkar, Mumbai, and IIM Kashipur, Vandana is also a certified ITIL Professional, Microsoft Certified Professional, and Certified Scrum Master. Her career journey includes leading enterprise-level cybersecurity programs at Symantec, Tech Mahindra, and Fujitsu, where she has developed and executed large-scale initiatives in Vulnerability Management, Endpoint Protection, SIEM (Security Information and Event Management), Exposure Management, IDAM, and Cloud Security.

Vandana's work has been grounded in both technology and empathy. Managing cybersecurity for global enterprises has taught her how to balance innovation with control, and speed with resilience. Beyond her corporate achievements, she is passionate about mentoring and empowering young girls to navigate the digital world safely.

Co-authoring this book with Mr. Anand Shinde, Vandana draws from both her professional expertise and her personal role as a mother to a daughter. Together, they wrote this book to raise awareness among girls and women about online privacy, digital hygiene, and the importance of protecting their digital identity in an ever-connected world.

For Vandana, cybersecurity is more than a profession-it's a mission. She believes that security is empowerment: it protects creativity, enables innovation, and builds trust in every digital interaction. Through this book, she extends that belief to every reader-especially young girls.

The Start of an Online Thriller

"Welcome to a world where the line between safety and danger is razor-thin, and every digital connection could be the start of something far darker than you ever imagined". Hacked and Hunted: A Smart Girl's Guide to Online Safety" invites you into the tense, high-stakes lives of three young women as they navigate the terrifying realities of the digital age.

In the blink of an eye, their seemingly normal lives are turned upside down by a hacker's malicious grip. What begins as innocent fun and online triumph quickly descends into a fight for survival-where every personal detail, every social post, and every click could be a step closer to disaster.

As you look into their journey, you'll find yourself caught in the web of cyber threats, phishing schemes, and dark corners of the internet where nothing is ever as it seems. But more than just a thrilling tale, this is a cautionary story that will leave you questioning everything about your online presence.

This book is for anyone who has ever trusted the digital world, for anyone who's felt the rush of sharing a moment online, and for anyone who's wondered what might happen when that trust is broken. Brace yourself, because once you step into this world, there's no turning back.

Chapter 1: Welcome to the Digital World

1.1 Introduction to Aarushi, Kaneera, and Sophia

Aarushi's laptop cast a soft glow across her face as she leaned closer, eyes narrowed in concentration. The vast world of tech, hidden patterns, and digital mysteries was often an impenetrable maze for others, but for Aarushi, it was pure magic-a puzzle waiting to be solved. She had been immersed in this digital world for as long as she could remember, inspired by her parents, both experts in online security, Aarushi had grown up with a fascination for the digital world. Conversations around keeping people safe online were common in her household, and her curiosity only grew from there, absorbing the language and concepts with ease. Watching her parents' dedication to keeping the digital world safe sparked her own passion to follow in their footsteps. For her, the world of tech and online safety wasn't just a career-it was a legacy, one she hoped to honor by making a difference in her own way.

Sophia:
Justice Seeker
Kaneera:
Social Media
Influencer
Aarushi:
Tech Geek

HER TWO BEST FRIENDS, Kaneera and Sophia, each brought their own unique talents and perspectives to their trio. Kaneera was Aarushi's polar opposite. With an outgoing personality and an influencer-level sense of style, Kaneera thrived in the spotlight. Her enthusiasm for life was infectious, and she often joked that the world was her stage. The daughter of a businessman and a dance teacher, Kaneera had grown up with the best of both worlds: her father's ambition and her mother's creative flair. Inspired by her mother's love for expression and performance, Kaneera had naturally gravitated toward social media as her platform. Her Instagram account was filled with photoshoots, beauty tutorials, and lifestyle content that resonated with her followers. She dreamed of hitting a million followers and believed that openness was the key to building her brand. To Aarushi's cautionary advice about oversharing, Kaneera would laugh and say, "Come on, what's the worst that could happen? It's just the internet!"

Sophia, the third pillar of their friendship, brought a quiet strength to the group. A level-headed law student, she was the voice of reason and justice. Her drive to protect others was fueled by a painful incident in her past-when a close relative had become a victim of fraud and identity theft. Watching her family struggle to regain control over their finances and sense of security had left a deep impression on Sophia. She vowed to use her knowledge to prevent similar incidents from happening to others. Law became her chosen path, and she was especially interested in privacy rights and digital ethics, issues she believed were crucial in a world where privacy could be compromised with a few clicks. She often spent late nights combing through case files and researching privacy laws, determined to make a difference.

Together, the three friends formed a well-balanced trio. Kaneera brought spontaneity, Aarushi was the strategist, and Sophia, ever grounded in her principles, served as the group's moral compass. They shared everything-inside jokes, dreams, and, soon enough, an unexpected journey into the shadowy and dangerous side of the internet.

The turning point in their lives arrived on a quiet autumn evening. Kaneera had just reached a follower milestone, and they were celebrating with a low-key night in, scrolling through her feed. "Look at this comment!" Kaneera giggled, showing her friends a message from a new follower. But as Aarushi glanced over, she felt a hint of unease. Some profiles commenting on Kaneera's posts seemed oddly repetitive, with similar, overly generic compliments.

The feeling pulled at her, but she brushed it off as overthinking. Yet, the subtle tension remained. Aarushi had learned from her parents to trust her instincts in matters of security, and she couldn't shake the sense that Kaneera's digital life was beginning to attract the wrong kind of attention.

AS THEY CELEBRATED Kaneera's reaching one million subscribers milestone that night, none of them realized that this small moment would soon mark the beginning of an uncharted journey. It would test their friendship, challenge Aarushi's skills, and expose Kaneera to a world where her openness was both her strength and her vulnerability. For Sophia, it would reveal the legal gaps that left people vulnerable to the digital age's hidden dangers.

The trio's lives were about to take a turn, pulling them deeper into the maze of online security threats, data vulnerabilities, and invisible risks lurking behind every screen. They were just three ordinary young women navigating life in an increasingly digital world. But soon, they'd learn that even the most harmless actions online could have profound, unexpected consequences.

As Kaneera, Aarushi, and Sophia settled into their routines, they grew more aware of the ways their lives were intertwined with the digital world. Each notification, post, and message subtly shaped their interactions, influencing how they were perceived both online and offline. This realization led them to discuss the often-overlooked importance of online security and digital privacy. Little did they know that these abstract concepts would soon become pressing priorities, as each new situation would reveal how easily seemingly harmless online actions could spiral into real-life problems.

1.2 The Importance of Online Security and Digital Privacy

T

he buzz of Kaneera's phone was a constant in their apartment, almost like background music to Aarushi's coding sessions. Each notification, new follower, or comment was a thrill for Kaneera, and she often checked her accounts without a second thought. But as Aarushi watched her friend live so freely online, she felt a growing need to address the invisible risks that came with it.

Aarushi knew that many people saw online security as something distant and technical, a responsibility for big corporations or governments, not something that applied to everyday life. But in reality, digital privacy affected everyone, and the stakes were personal. Behind each tap and swipe, there was potential exposure, and without the right awareness, people unknowingly shared far more than they intended.

"A lot of people think online security is just about preventing data theft," Aarushi explained one day as they sat in their shared kitchen. "But it's really about protecting your entire identity-your reputation, your safety, and your peace of mind. It's about making sure that someone else doesn't gain control over your life."

Kaneera raised an eyebrow. "My life isn't that interesting. Who'd care enough to hack me?"

"That's the thing," Aarushi said, leaning forward. "Online security isn't just about interest; it's about access. Once someone has even a tiny bit of your personal information, like your birthdate or email, they can piece together a lot about you. And if they want to, they can use it in ways you'd never expect."

Sophia joined in, always ready to add her perspective. "Think about it, Kaneera. Companies track everything we do online-where we shop, what we watch, and even what we read. They use it to sell ads, sure, but that's just the beginning. In the wrong hands, that information can turn into targeted harassment or worse."

The room grew quiet. Kaneera frowned, glancing at her phone. She'd never thought of her posts, her likes, or her comments as pieces of a puzzle that could be used against her. It had always seemed harmless-after all, everyone was online. But now, with her rising follower count and Aarushi's cautionary words echoing in her mind, she felt a chill.

"The thing is, you don't need to be a famous person or a big company to be targeted," Aarushi continued. "Everyday people like you and me are targeted every day. It's about being aware of what could happen and taking steps to prevent it." She thought of the headlines she'd read in tech forums about data breaches, identity theft, and accounts being hacked. Each story was a reminder that everyone was vulnerable, especially those who didn't believe they could ever be a target.

"And digital privacy?" Sophia added. "It's our right to keep certain things to ourselves. Just because we live in a hyperconnected world doesn't mean we need to let everyone in. Privacy is what keeps us safe, and it's worth protecting."

Aarushi nodded, pleased to see Sophia resonating with the point. "Exactly. Imagine a house. You wouldn't leave all the windows open and your front door unlocked just because you live in a safe neighbourhood, right? The internet is like an open world with many hidden dangers. It's a huge opportunity but also a huge risk."

Kaneera looked thoughtful. "But can't we just set our profiles to private and be safe?"

"To some extent, yes," Aarushi replied. "But privacy settings can only do so much. True digital privacy is more than just setting up barriers; it's about being mindful of what we share and understanding how that data can be used."

Sophia added, "Privacy is also about controlling our own narrative. It's choosing what people see and, more importantly, what they don't. It's about empowerment." She smiled, knowing she was in her element discussing this. For her, privacy was a part of dignity and respect, something worth fighting for.

That night, as Kaneera scrolled through her photos and posts, her view of online security had changed. She started seeing each post as a piece of her identity, a glimpse of her life that she was sharing with the world. She wondered just how much of her was floating in the digital world, and for the first time, she felt a mix of pride and fear.

For Aarushi, this was just the beginning of what she hoped would be a larger conversation. She wanted Kaneera to understand that in a world where every like post, and click could be tracked, everyone was responsible for safeguarding their own digital space. For Aarushi, protecting digital privacy wasn't just a skill; it was a mission, a way of showing those she cared about that safety was worth the effort.

Online security and digital privacy weren't just abstract concepts-they were as real as locking the door at night, as essential as wearing a seatbelt. In a world where the digital could affect the physical, knowing how to secure oneself online was becoming an essential skill.

As the three friends sat together, they realized that their digital lives weren't just theirs alone. They were part of a more extensive network, a vast web of connections where everyone was connected. And while that could be a wonderful thing, it could also mean danger if one wasn't careful. Kaneera and Sophia looked at Aarushi, each appreciating in their own way that her quiet caution would keep them safe as they embarked deeper into the digital world.

With their newfound understanding of digital privacy, Aarushi, Kaneera, and Sophia start paying closer attention to the small signs that something might be amiss in their online spaces. What was once routine-simple posts, casual messages, and geotags-now appears under a new, more cautious lens. Each of them, in their way, begins to notice subtle red flags, from unexpected messages to oddly specific comments from strangers. It's only a matter of time before they face their first true encounter with the implications of oversharing and cyber vulnerability, and each friend must handle these risks as they unfold in unexpected and personal ways.

1.3 How they Encounter Early Signs of Online Threats in their Lives

It started subtly, so subtly that only Aarushi noticed the tiny digital "cracks" forming in Kaneera's online life. Sitting at their kitchen table one evening, Kaneera showed off her latest Instagram post, delighting in the excitement of her climbing follower count. Her notifications buzzed every few seconds, each one a mix of likes, comments, and new followers. But something caught Aarushi's eye-certain comments seemed... off.

"CONGRATS ON THE NEW post," one comment read, but it was from a profile with no name or photo, just a string of random numbers and letters.

Another profile chimed in, "You're getting famous fast, Kaneera," repeating the exact same message as three others above it. It wasn't just one or two strange profiles-there were dozens. Aarushi's curiosity turned to concern. "Kaneera, have you noticed these bot-like accounts popping up lately?"

Kaneera smiled, scrolling past them. "Yeah, they're annoying, but it's normal, right? Big influencers get fake followers all the time."

"Maybe," Aarushi replied, her mind racing. "But it could also mean someone's tracking your activity or trying to spam your account." She made a mental note to look into the profiles more deeply when she had a moment.

Sophia, who'd been reading on the couch, looked up. "It sounds harmless for now, but we all know how these things can escalate." As a law intern, Sophia had recently come across cases involving cyber harassment and identity theft, which made her doubtful. To her, these things weren't just numbers on a screen; they were potential red flags.

Later that week, the mysterious feeling grew. Kaneera received an official email from a brand wanting to sponsor her social media posts. "Check this out!" she said, her excitement evident as she forwarded the message to Aarushi. This could be huge!"

The email seemed legitimate at first glance, with the brand's logo and links to its website. But Aarushi's instincts told her something was off. The brand's email domain didn't match the official website-just one subtle difference that most people wouldn't notice. The email asked Kaneera to "click here to verify your account," followed by a password request.

"Kaneera, don't click that link," Aarushi warned quickly. She looked at her friend with an intensity that surprised even her. "This is what's called phishing. They want you to enter your password so they can hack into your account."

Kaneera's excitement faded as she looked from her laptop screen to Aarushi, her confidence shaken. "But it looks so real... Why would anyone target me?"

"Because they don't see 'Kaneera'-they see an account with a lot of followers, someone they can manipulate for profit," Aarushi explained. "Cyber attackers are getting better at creating realistic messages. All it takes is one click, and they can take over your account or even access your personal information."

Sophia stared. "And if they're able to control your account, they can post anything they want, pretending to be you. It's like giving someone the keys to your life."

Just as they thought they were in the clear, the situation intensified. A few days later, Aarushi noticed something strange on her own laptop. Her webcam light flickered on for a split second, then went dark. She froze, staring at the tiny light as her mind raced through possible explanations. Had she accidentally clicked a setting? Was it a glitch?

But deep down, she knew better. After weeks of helping Kaneera spot suspicious activity, Aarushi recognized a potential intrusion when she saw one. Someone had accessed her camera remotely.

"Aarushi, you okay?" Kaneera asked, noticing her sudden silence.

Aarushi took a deep breath, her hands hovering over her keyboard. "I think someone's watching me." She quickly scanned her system, looking for any unfamiliar programs that could have given someone remote access. It didn't take long before she found the culprit-a hidden spyware program quietly running in the background, capturing everything she did on her screen.

She looked up at Kaneera and Sophia, both of them now watching her with wide eyes. "This is serious. Someone installed spyware on my laptop."

Kaneera shocked. "Wait, like... someone could see everything you've been doing?"

Aarushi nodded, her voice calm but her mind racing. "Yes. Spyware like this can record keystrokes, access my files, and even turn on my camera. This isn't just an inconvenience-this is someone invading my privacy in real-time."

Sophia's face darkened. "This is more than creepy. This is a crime." Her hands clenched as if she were already preparing a case in her mind. "Whoever's behind this isn't just a troll; they're deliberately targeting us."

Aarushi deleted the spyware, feeling fear as she realized the scope of what they were dealing with. "We're not just random girls online anymore. Someone is going out of their way to mess with us."

The incidents continued over the next few weeks-unfamiliar IP addresses attempting to log into their accounts, strange pop-up ads, and even random calls and messages from unknown numbers. Each sign pointed to something bigger, something darker stalking beneath the surface of their online lives.

As Aarushi, Kaneera, and Sophia pieced together the signs, they came to a terrible realization. These weren't isolated incidents or harmless pranks. They were being targeted, and the attacks were escalating. Someone, somewhere, was watching, waiting, and ready to use every weakness they exposed online.

And as they locked eyes, they knew they couldn't just brush it off. They needed to be attentive, informed and prepared-because this was only the beginning.

As Kaneera, Aarushi, and Sophia become more mindful of their digital footprint, each friend takes a closer look at their own online habits. They recognize that even casual posts can unintentionally reveal personal details and that every "like," tag, or geotag carries its risks. Kaneera's journey into social media stardom is just beginning, and she's thrilled to be building an audience, unaware of the unique challenges that lie ahead. As she eagerly dives into the world of social media, Kaneera will soon realize that her newfound fame brings with it an unexpected dark side-one that even her closest friends couldn't have anticipated. Her digital life is about to open doors she never meant to, and the consequences will unfold in ways that challenge her sense of safety and control.

Chapter 2: The Social Media Trap

2.1 Kaneera's Rise as a Social Media Influencer

Kaneera's first video to go viral was a total accident. She'd been recording a casual skincare routine in their tiny apartment bathroom, balancing her phone on a stack of textbooks to get the right angle. A few quick edits and a funny caption later, she posted it online, figuring it might get a few laughs from friends. By the next morning, her phone was buzzing nonstop with notifications-likes, comments, and new followers pouring in from every corner of the internet.

"This is insane!" Kaneera screamed, spinning around in the kitchen as her notifications climbed. She turned to Aarushi, wide-eyed and smiling. "I think I'm actually going viral!"

AARUSHI GAVE HER AN amused smile, looking up from her laptop. "Congrats, Kaneera. Just remember to keep some things private, alright?"

But Kaneera was too busy celebrating to hear her friend's warning fully. As her follower count skyrocketed, so did her ambition. What started as a small following of college friends and family quickly expanded into a vast community of people eager for Kaneera's advice on everything from skincare to study tips. With each post, she improved her style, finding the perfect balance of personal stories, humor, and genuine recommendations that kept her audience hooked.

Her unique charm and unfiltered personality made her relatable. Soon enough, brands started to notice her, reaching out with offers for collaborations and sponsorships. A brand deal here, a sponsored post there-Kaneera's social media presence was no longer just a hobby; it was becoming a career. The thrill of being recognized and appreciated by complete strangers was intoxicating, and Kaneera couldn't get enough.

Sophia watched Kaneera's rise with a mix of admiration and concern. "It's amazing how quickly your account is growing, Kaneera," she commented one evening, scrolling through Kaneera's feed. "But just remember, you're putting a lot of yourself out there."

Kaneera brushed it off with a laugh. "It's all harmless! My followers are the best. And besides, what's the point of being an influencer if you're not... you know, influencing?"

Aarushi raised an eyebrow. "Just be careful. The more you share, the more people feel like they know you. Sometimes, they think they know you a little too well."

But Kaneera couldn't resist the charm of her growing platform. She loved connecting with her followers and felt a sense of duty to share her life authentically. When her follower count hit fifty thousand, Kaneera organized a "day in my life" series on her stories, walking her audience through her favourite spots around town-her morning coffee place, her favourite bookstore, and the park where she loved to jog. Her followers ate it up, sending messages of encouragement and flooding her DMs with questions about her routine.

At first, the comments were all positive, filled with compliments and friendly questions. But as Kaneera's popularity grew, the tone of her inbox started to change. People began asking personal questions about her friends, her schedule, and even her whereabouts. Strangers would comment on her posts, mentioning things she hadn't shared, as if they'd pieced together parts of her life from the little details she'd let slip over time.

Then came the fan accounts. Some were sweet, filled with curated pictures of Kaneera and cute captions. But others felt intrusive-someone even reposted photos of her family that she'd shared in passing. One account in particular started tagging her in posts with screenshots of her stories, dissecting every detail and speculating about her personal life.

"Look at this," Kaneera showed Aarushi, half laughing, half uneasy, as she pointed to one of the posts. "It's like they're documenting my every move!"

Aarushi frowned, a shadow of concern crossing her face. "Kaneera, this isn't just fandom anymore. These people are tracking your life like it's a TV show. It's a little... unsettling, don't you think?"

Kaneera brushed it off, though deep down, she couldn't deny the hint of discomfort that had begun to creep in. The thrill of fame was intoxicating, but there was something strange about knowing that complete strangers felt so connected to her and had taken such an interest in her daily routine.

But the line between admiration and obsession continued to blur. The higher her follower count climbed, the more her digital world felt like a glass house, with every detail of her life on display. Some followers would DM her multiple times a day, each message more intrusive than the last. A few even speculated about her "secrets," guessing her class schedule, hometown, or favourite restaurants with creepy accuracy.

One night, after a particularly unnerving DM from someone claiming they'd seen her at the grocery store, Kaneera confided in Sophia. "I don't get it. I mean, I put myself out there, sure, but I didn't ask for all this... attention. Why can't they just like my posts and move on?"

Sophia sighed, placing a comforting hand on Kaneera's shoulder. "You're an open book, Kaneera. People think that because they see parts of your life, they're entitled to the rest. But you don't owe them anything beyond what you choose to share."

Aarushi joined the conversation, her face serious. "This is exactly why I worry about oversharing. When you let people see into your life, some will take it as an invitation to pry further. And not everyone has good intentions."

Kaneera felt the pain of realization, remembering all the times she'd posted photos with geotags, listed her favourite places, and shared details about her routine without a second thought. The pieces of her life that once felt fun and harmless now seemed like breadcrumbs, clues that anyone could follow. She started to see the risks that Aarushi had warned her about, risks that went beyond the screen and into her real life.

But the appeal of fame was strong, and despite her friends' concerns, Kaneera continued to post-after all, she loved what she did, and her followers were still mostly supportive. She just hoped that this uncomfortable feeling in her gut would pass.

Unknown to Kaneera, however, her rise to social media stardom had caught the eye of someone who didn't just want to follow her life from afar. This person, stalking behind a screen, saw Kaneera not as a personality to support but as a puzzle to solve. And as Kaneera's life continued to play out online, they were quietly collecting every piece, preparing for a game Kaneera had no idea she was a part of.

As Kaneera's popularity surges, her online persona evolves, bringing her an exciting new audience but also introducing a sense of exposure she hadn't anticipated. What was once just a fun hobby of sharing moments has turned into a lifestyle that thousands of people tune into daily. But the attention isn't always positive, and soon Kaneera realizes that her openness has drawn more than just friendly followers. Strange messages and invasive comments begin appearing, hinting at something darker stalking beneath her social media success. Now, she faces the challenge of balancing her public persona with the very real need to protect her personal space.

2.2 First Signs of Cyberstalking and Oversharing Risks

It started with small, unsettling coincidences-things Kaneera could almost laugh off at first. As her follower count increased, her inbox filled with messages from all over, some cheering her on, others sharing their own stories. But now and then, a comment would pop up that felt a little too personal, a little too close to home, like a follower who mentioned her favorite coffee shop with weird familiarity or another who asked if she'd be visiting her "usual jogging spot" that evening.

Kaneera tried to ignore it, chalking it up to fans who were just really into her content. But soon, the comments became more frequent, blending admiration with something else, something that made her feel exposed. One day, as she shared a story at her favorite café, a direct message appeared on her screen within seconds. The sender, a follower she didn't recognize-asked if she was enjoying her latte, mentioning the exact drink she'd ordered.

Kaneera, you're being cyberstalked!
Aarushi, how does he know what I drank?
Enjoying the Latte!

"LOOK AT THIS!" KANEERA said, showing the message to Aarushi, "This guy somehow knew what I was drinking... That's creepy, right?"

Aarushi's expression grew serious. "Kaneera, this isn't just 'creepy.' If someone's tracking your every move, it's more than just a fan. You might be dealing with someone who's cyberstalking you."

The word hit Kaneera hard. Cyberstalking. She'd read about it before, but it was something that happened to other people, not her. "But... I don't share anything that personal, do I?"

Sophia, who'd just entered the room, overheard and pulled up Kaneera's social media page. "Kaneera, you do post a lot of details about your life. Even small things, like the view from your favorite café or jogging routes, can give people enough clues to piece together a map of your daily routine."

Aarushi nodded. "Cyberstalkers are good at reading between the lines. Even if you don't tell them outright, they can connect the dots. They follow patterns."

Kaneera's mind raced as she considered her recent posts. She hadn't thought much of sharing details about her routines or tagging her favorite spots-after all, it's what influencers did. Her followers loved getting glimpses into her day-to-day life, and she'd always seen it as harmless, part of her brand. But now, the sense of unease she'd been pushing aside began to take hold.

That night, as Kaneera scrolled through her DMs, she noticed something strange. A series of messages from a follower she didn't recognize, each more persistent than the last. The messages started innocently enough-a quick compliment, a few questions about her content. But over time, they had become intrusive, filled with personal details about Kaneera's schedule and whereabouts that she'd never explicitly shared. She felt her heart race as she read one message: "Saw you on your morning jog again today! Loved the red jacket."

Her hands shook as she reread the message. She hadn't told anyone about her new jacket, and she certainly hadn't mentioned her jogging schedule online. "How did they know?" she whispered, feeling a chill run down her spine.

Sophia, always one to offer perspective, reassured her, "The thing about social media, Kaneera, is that people feel like they know you. But some take that feeling too far, thinking they're part of your life without ever having met you."

Aarushi, who'd been silently listening, spoke up. "Kaneera, this is exactly why I keep telling you about oversharing. People can take seemingly harmless details and turn them into a pattern. And once they have a pattern, they can follow it-sometimes literally."

Kaneera looked at her phone, a sense of worry washing over her. "But what can I do? I don't want to stop posting. My followers expect me to share my life with them."

Aarushi placed a reassuring hand on her shoulder. "You don't have to stop. But you can control what you share. Be strategic. Share things after the fact, blur out your surroundings, or don't tag specific places until after you've left. You don't have to give up your privacy for the sake of your brand."

The conversation remained with Kaneera, and she started noticing other red flags she'd previously ignored. The way certain accounts would comment on posts within seconds of her uploading them, often asking oddly specific questions. The fact that some followers seemed to be cross-referencing her stories, piecing together her schedule based on past posts. For the first time, she began to see her online presence from a different perspective-not just as a brand but as a potential vulnerability.

A few days later, another incident rattled her further. Kaneera received a direct message from an account with no profile picture, just a string of numbers as a username. The message was a warning: "Careful what you post, Kaneera. Not everyone who follows you is a fan." Her blood ran cold. She showed the message to Aarushi, her voice barely a whisper. "Is this... is this real?"

Aarushi's face hardened. "It could be a troll, but with everything else that's happened, we can't ignore it. Someone is going out of their way to make you feel unsafe. We need to be proactive about this."

Sophia, with her legal knowledge, suggested Kaneera start documenting everything-the strange comments, the overly personal messages, and now this cryptic warning. "If this escalates, we'll need evidence to take action. Cyberstalking is a crime, Kaneera. Don't let anyone make you feel like this is your fault or that you're overreacting."

Feeling the weight of her friends' support, Kaneera took a deep breath. She decided to take immediate steps to protect herself, starting with a review of her account settings. She made her profile private, temporarily disabling the location tags she'd once used so freely. Her next posts would come with added discretion, a new awareness that sharing her life didn't have to mean sacrificing her safety.

As Kaneera adapted to her new approach, she realized that her online identity could still thrive without giving everything away. With Aarushi's guidance, she implemented privacy controls she hadn't previously considered. From two-factor authentication to limiting who could comment on her posts, Kaneera started rebuilding her digital world with security in mind.

But even as Kaneera took these steps, a bothering feeling persisted-the sense that someone was still watching, still stalking in the background. Online security was no longer just a theoretical concept to her. It was natural, urgent, and personal. She couldn't shake the thought that the "fans" she once saw as harmless could, under the right circumstances, become something far more sinister.

And somewhere out there, the person behind that warning message was watching her every move, waiting for the moment she let her guard down.

What began as a thrill-the rapid growth of her online presence-starts to feel more like an invasion. Kaneera's casual online shares have unwittingly given strangers a roadmap to her life. The subtle signs of oversharing grow into more pronounced incidents, each one leaving her increasingly wary. But this is only the beginning. As her digital fame continues to grow, Kaneera starts to encounter more of social media's shadowy side, from trolling to invasive comments, and she realizes that her personal privacy is more vulnerable than she ever imagined.

2.3 The Dark Side of Social Media: Trolling, Privacy Leaks, and Reputation Damage

As Kaneera's popularity continued to climb, she felt like she was finally living the dream she'd once only imagined. Brands wanted to collaborate, followers constantly engaged with her content, and each post seemed to bring her closer to her goal of a million followers. But with her rising fame, Kaneera began experiencing an unexpected side of social media-one she hadn't prepared for.

It began subtly, almost like background noise. Amid the positive comments, Kaneera noticed a few negative remarks slipping in, each harsher than the last. At first, she brushed them off, blaming it on jealousy or people simply having a bad day. But as days passed, the comments became more vicious, more personal.

"FAKE INFLUENCER," ONE comment read. Another mocked her appearance, and others even speculated on her relationships, accusing her of fabricating aspects of her life to get more views. Her excitement turned to fear and anger each time she checked her notifications, knowing that each post might attract not just her fans but a swarm of anonymous critics eager to tear her down.

Aarushi noticed Kaneera's shift in mood and suggested that she take a break from social media. "Kaneera, sometimes it's better to take a step back. Trolling is just part of this online world, and it has nothing to do with you."

Kaneera sighed, visibly frustrated. "I get that people can be mean, but it feels like they're trying to ruin everything I've worked for. They don't even know me, but they're acting like I owe them something."

Sophia, ever the realist, nodded in agreement. "People can be cruel online because it's easy to hide behind a screen. It's a lot harder to see the impact their words have when they don't see your face."

But the trolls weren't the only problem. A few weeks later, Kaneera's world was rocked when a friend messaged her, saying that her private information had been shared on a gossip forum. Someone had leaked her full name, hometown, and even the university she attended. The post detailed parts of her life that

Kaneera had never shared online, creating a mix of truth and falsehoods that painted her in an unflattering light.

Her stomach dropped as she read through the forum thread, each comment more invasive than the last. Users speculated about her background, spread rumors about her relationships, and shared wild theories about her family. Some commenters went so far as to dig through her old posts, pulling out details to support their assumptions. In a single post, everything she thought she controlled about her online presence was stripped away.

"Why are they doing this?" Kaneera asked, her voice barely above a whisper as she showed the forum thread to Aarushi and Sophia. Her friends looked at the screen in shock, unable to comprehend the cruelty.

"They're just strangers, Kaneera," Aarushi said, trying to comfort her. "But they don't know you. They're projecting their own issues onto you because it's easier than looking at themselves."

Sophia added, "Unfortunately, this is the reality for anyone in the public eye. The more people feel they know you, the more entitled they feel to judge you, even if their opinions are completely unfounded."

Kaneera shook her head, her hands trembling. "But this is my life. They're spreading lies about me and making me out to be someone I'm not. It's like they've stolen my identity."

This feeling of vulnerability reached a new level when a stranger emailed Kaneera with screenshots of her private messages, including chats with close friends and even family members. Somehow, someone had hacked into her account, accessing her personal conversations and using them as a weapon. "Just a little preview," the email read, taunting her. "Keep your fans entertained, or we'll leak everything."

Kaneera's heart pounded. It was one thing to face trolls and rumors, but this felt different. Her privacy had been breached, and she no longer felt safe, even in her own digital space.

When Kaneera showed the email to her friends, both Aarushi and Sophia reacted with shock and anger. "This isn't just trolling anymore," Aarushi said, her voice tense. "This is targeted harassment. Whoever did this is trying to control you, to make you feel powerless."

Sophia leaned forward, her expression serious. "This is a form of blackmail, Kaneera. If they're threatening to leak more, they're actively trying to ruin your reputation. We need to find out how they got into your account."

They spent the evening combing through Kaneera's social media accounts, checking for signs of a security breach. Aarushi guided Kaneera in changing her passwords, setting up two-factor authentication, and reviewing the devices connected to her accounts. But even as they worked, Kaneera couldn't shake the feeling of helplessness.

"Everyone warned me that the internet could be a dangerous place, but I thought that was for people who shared secrets or did something wrong," Kaneera murmured. "I didn't think that just living my life online would make me a target."

Aarushi nodded sympathy in her eyes. "Social media has a dark side, Kaneera. When people feel anonymous, they forget that their actions have consequences. For them, it's a game. But for you, it's your life."

Sophia added, "This is reputation damage, Kaneera, and it's not fair. But we'll get through it. You have every right to fight for your privacy and to be respected online."

The incident forced Kaneera to reassess her relationship with her online presence. She had always seen social media as an exciting space to connect, share, and grow. But now, she saw its other side-the side that demanded boundaries, caution, and sometimes, distance.

As Kaneera looked at her friends, she felt a renewed sense of purpose. She wouldn't let trolls, privacy leaks, or hackers define her. But from that day on, she decided to take her privacy and security more seriously, understanding that not everyone who followed her journey was cheering her on.

In the quiet that followed, Kaneera realized something important: the internet wasn't just a place of opportunity; it was a place where her personal safety and reputation could be tested at any moment. And if she wanted to keep her identity intact, she needed to protect herself-no matter the cost.

The deeper Kaneera experiences the world of online fame, the more complicated it becomes. The supportive comments she initially received have been overshadowed by trolling, privacy leaks, and a growing unease that her life is no longer entirely her own. As she struggles to balance her public image with her private self, Kaneera learns that the risks extend far beyond her personal accounts. She's now facing a reality where her online reputation can be threatened at any moment, and it's becoming clear that her online life affects not just her but her relationships with Aarushi, Sophia, and even her followers. With the harsh realities of social media casting a shadow over her life, Kaneera and her friends prepare to explore the complexities of online security, diving into the various types of online threats that anyone can face-and discovering just how much is at stake.

Chapter 3: Phishing for Trouble

3.1 Aarushi Discovers Suspicious Activity on Kaneera's Account

It all began when Aarushi received a direct message from Kaneera, a message that felt oddly out of place. The tone wasn't quite Kaneera's usual friendly chatter. Instead, it was short, with a link attached and a quick note: "Hey, you have to check this out. Trust me!" Aarushi's curiosity was piqued, but something about it didn't sit right with her. The message seemed too brief, and Kaneera usually added a bit of context with any link she shared.

Rather than clicking right away, Aarushi decided to reach out to Kaneera directly. She called, and Kaneera answered almost immediately. "Hey! What's up?" Kaneera said cheerfully.

"DID YOU JUST SEND ME a message with a link?" Aarushi asked, suspicion lacing her tone.

There was a pause. "A link? No... wait, what kind of link?"

Aarushi explained the message, and silence grew on the other end of the line. "I didn't send that," Kaneera replied, worry creeping into her voice. "Could someone be using my account?"

Together, they logged into Kaneera's social media account, where Aarushi noticed something else odd: the message had been sent to several other people in Kaneera's contacts list, not just her. It seemed like Kaneera's account had been accessed by someone else-someone trying to spread links under her name.

"I think your account's been compromised, Kaneera," Aarushi said, her tone serious. "It could be a phishing attempt or something worse."

Kaneera groaned, her mind racing. "But I thought I was careful! I use a strong password, and I never share my login information. How did this happen?"

They spent the next few minutes combing through Kaneera's activity log, spotting more signs of suspicious activity-login attempts from strange locations, messages she hadn't sent, and even a few posts she didn't remember making. The more they dug, the clearer it became: someone had managed to get access to her account, sending out phishing links to her followers disguised as messages from her.

"What's phishing exactly?" Kaneera asked, feeling a bit lost as she scrolled through her account's activity log.

Aarushi explained, "It's when someone pretends to be you or a trustworthy source, usually to get people to click on a link. That link might lead to a fake login page that tries to steal personal information, or it could even download malware onto the device. It's all about tricking people into giving up their data."

"Lovely," Kaneera muttered. "So now my friends think I'm trying to scam them?"

"Not exactly, but we should act fast," Aarushi replied. "The longer this goes on, the more it could damage your reputation and even lead to something worse. Phishing attacks can lead to identity theft, financial losses, or further access to other accounts if the hackers get hold of passwords."

They wasted no time setting Kaneera's account to private and changing her password to something more complex. Aarushi also suggested that Kaneera enable two-factor authentication (2FA) to add an extra layer of security. "With 2FA, even if someone has your password, they won't be able to log in without a code sent to your phone. It's like having a second lock on the door."

Kaneera nodded, grateful for Aarushi's guidance. But there was one more thing gnawing at her. "If this happened to me, could it happen to others? I don't want my friends falling for this."

Together, they went through Kaneera's contact list, identifying everyone who had received the suspicious message. Aarushi drafted a warning message that Kaneera could send to each person, explaining the situation and advising them not to click the link. They hoped that a quick response would limit the damage, but Kaneera couldn't shake the feeling of exposure. Her personal space had been invaded, her name used as a tool for something malicious. When the immediate fixes were complete, they sat back, exhausted but determined. Kaneera spoke up, "You know, I've always heard about these things, but I never thought it would happen to me. I mean, it's just social media, right?"

Aarushi smiled knowingly. "A lot of people think that, Kaneera. But social media accounts are often linked to email, sometimes even to bank accounts or other important information. Hackers use phishing because it works, and they prey on the fact that people don't think it'll happen to them. The best thing we can do is stay alert."

As Kaneera processed this, a new question dawned on her. "What about other kinds of phishing? I mean, if they can use my social media, what else can they do?"

Aarushi's expression turned thoughtful. "Phishing has different forms. There's email phishing, where they send fake emails that look like they're from your bank or a trusted source. Then there's 'spear-phishing,' which is targeted at specific individuals or companies, often with very personalized information. It's not just random-it's designed to look authentic."

The more they discussed it, the clearer it became to Kaneera that phishing wasn't just about one hacked account. It was a serious threat that could affect anyone, and without knowing the signs, many people would fall victim. She resolved to be more cautious and to help her friends stay alert, too.

Kaneera felt a renewed sense of awareness and caution, but the incident stayed with her, making her rethink her online presence. She wondered if other threats were creeping into her digital life, risks she hadn't yet noticed. As she delved deeper, Kaneera would soon discover that phishing was just one piece of a much larger puzzle, and the online world was far more intricate than she'd ever imagined.

3.2 Explanation of Phishing Attacks and How They Happen

As Kaneera and Aarushi discussed the suspicious activity on Kaneera's account, Aarushi decided it was time to discuss phishing in depth. She wanted Kaneera to understand how these attacks work, not only to prevent future breaches but also to build a strong foundation for digital awareness.

"Phishing isn't just about hacking accounts," Aarushi began. "It's about deceiving people by impersonating trusted sources, usually to get them to click a link, open an attachment, or give away sensitive information."

KANEERA LISTENED INTENTLY, nodding as Aarushi continued. "Think of phishing as a scam where the attacker pretends to be someone they're not, like a bank, a friend, or even a government agency. They use fake messages, often through email or social media, that look really convincing. If you fall for it and click on the link, you could be taken to a fake website that looks real but isn't. There, they might ask for your username, password, or even credit card details."

"But how do they make it look so real?" Kaneera asked, her brows furrowing. "I mean, wouldn't it be obvious that it's a fake?"

Aarushi explained, "Not always. Phishers are good at making these emails and messages look legitimate. They use logos, official-sounding language, and sometimes even personal information they've gathered about you from public profiles. For example, if a hacker knows your bank with 'XYZ Bank,' they might send you an email that looks like it's from that bank, asking you to verify your account information. They're counting on the fact that people won't double-check the email address or think twice about clicking the link."

Kaneera shook, realizing how easy it would be to fall for something like that. "So, all it takes is one click, and they have access to everything?"

"Exactly," Aarushi replied. "Sometimes clicking the link is enough to download malware onto your device. Other times, they'll send you to a fake login page. They call this 'spoofing,' where they copy the design of real websites so well that people don't realize it's a fake. You log in, and bam-they have your password."

"Why would someone go through all that trouble?" Kaneera wondered aloud.

"Phishing attacks are incredibly profitable," Aarushi explained. "Some attackers are after money, trying to access bank accounts or credit cards. Others want personal data they can sell on the dark web, like Social Security numbers, which can be used for identity theft. And sometimes, it's about corporate spying, where hackers target companies to steal trade secrets or financial information."

Aarushi went on to explain different forms of phishing, highlighting how varied and sophisticated these attacks could be:

- **Email Phishing:** The most common type of phishing, where an attacker sends a fake email to a target, often disguised as a message from a bank, a trusted company, or even a friend. "If you ever get an email with a link that seems off or an unexpected attachment, always be suspicious," she advised. "Check the sender's email address carefully. Phishers often use addresses that are similar to real ones but with small variations like missing letters or extra numbers."

- **Spear Phishing:** A more targeted approach where attackers gather information about a specific person to make the phishing message more believable. "For instance," Aarushi said, "if a hacker knows you work for a certain company, they might send you an email pretending to be from a colleague or your boss. They might even use your real name and job title to gain your trust."
- **Whaling:** Similar to spear phishing but targeting high-profile individuals, like executives or celebrities. "With whaling, phishers go after big players, hoping to gain access to sensitive information from high-level accounts."
- **Smishing and Vishing:** Phishing attacks aren't limited to email. "Smishing" involves fake SMS messages, often with a sense of urgency-like claiming your account is locked, and you need to verify your identity immediately. "Vishing," on the other hand, is voice phishing, where scammers call you pretending to be from tech support or a government agency. "They rely on fear and urgency to make you act without thinking," Aarushi warned.
- **Clone Phishing:** In this form of phishing, attackers create a nearly identical copy of a legitimate email the target has received before. The message is cloned, with only the link or attachment altered to redirect the victim to a malicious site. "Since you might have seen the original email before, it's easy to fall for it if you don't realize this one's been modified," she explained.

As Kaneera absorbed all this information, she felt a mix of disbelief and anxiety. "It's scary to think these things happen so often. I mean, anyone could be a target."

"Yes, and it's not just you," Aarushi emphasized. "Phishers often use social media or professional networking sites to gather personal information. They look for any detail they can use to make their attacks more convincing. That's why it's so important to be careful about what you share online."

Aarushi continued, "And remember, phishers play on emotions. They might create a sense of urgency, like 'Act now before your account gets locked!' or use a friendly tone, pretending to be someone you know. They're counting on people acting without thinking, especially if the message appears to come from a trusted source."

"Wow, I never realized there were so many types of phishing," Kaneera said, a little overwhelmed but grateful for the knowledge. "So what should I do if I ever think I'm being phished?"

Aarushi offered some essential tips:

- **Be suspicious:** If you receive an unexpected message, don't rush. Look for signs that the message might be fake.
- **Verify the source:** Contact the person or company through a trusted method, not by replying to the suspicious message.
- **Check for red flags:** Look for spelling errors, strange email addresses, and unusual language.
- **Hover over links:** On a computer, hover your mouse over a link before clicking to see where it really leads.
- **Enable two-factor authentication:** This adds an extra layer of security, so even if someone steals your password, they can't access your account without the second factor.

Listening intently, Kaneera realized how easily someone could fall into a phishing trap without even knowing it. "Thanks, Aarushi. I feel like I'm finally seeing the full picture."

"Glad to help," Aarushi replied with a smile. "Phishing attacks can be sneaky, but once you know what to look for, you're already a step ahead. Being aware and cautious can make a huge difference."

With a clearer understanding of phishing tactics, Kaneera felt more empowered, but the experience left her curious about what other online dangers might be waiting for. Phishing was just one of many tricks hackers used, and as they explored further, Kaneera and her friends would uncover even more hidden risks in the digital world-risks that could affect anyone who wasn't prepared.

3.3 Aarushi Explains How to Spot Phishing Attempts

After learning about the different types of phishing, Kaneera was more cautious but also a bit overwhelmed. She had a million questions swirling in her mind, so Aarushi decided to break it down further, focusing on specific signs to watch out for in potential phishing attempts. They sat together over coffee, with Kaneera eager to learn the tools to help her identify suspicious messages before they could cause any harm.

"ALRIGHT, KANEERA," Aarushi began, "the key to avoiding phishing is to know the red flags. Once you're familiar with them, you'll be able to spot phishing attempts more easily. Let's go over a few signs to watch for in emails, messages, or even social media DMs."

1. Check the Sender's Address Carefully: "Phishing emails usually come from strange or fake email addresses," Aarushi explained. "A lot of the time, they'll look similar to a real address, but they might have extra letters, numbers, or slight misspellings. For instance, you might get an email from 'support@ammazon.com' instead of 'support@amazon.com.' Those small differences are easy to miss if you're not looking closely."

Kaneera nodded, taking mental notes. "So, always double-check the sender's address?"

"Exactly," Aarushi confirmed. "If you see anything unusual or if the address doesn't look right, it's a huge red flag."

2. Look for Urgent or Threatening Language: "Phishing messages often try to scare you into acting quickly," Aarushi continued. "They might say things like, 'Your account will be locked unless you respond immediately!' or 'Verify your information now to avoid suspension!' They want you to panic and react before you think."

Kaneera thought back to messages she'd received in the past. "That makes sense. When you're in a rush, it's easy to act without double-checking."

"Exactly," Aarushi replied. "Real companies rarely use threatening language like that. If it seems like they're trying to make you panic, take a step back and verify the source first."

3. Check for Generic Greetings: "Phishing emails often use generic greetings, like 'Dear Customer' or 'Valued User,'" Aarushi explained. "They rarely use your real name. Real companies usually address you personally, especially if it's something important. So if you see a generic greeting, it's worth being cautious."

"But what if it does have my name?" Kaneera asked.

"It's possible for more advanced phishing emails to use your name," Aarushi admitted, "but it's still less common. If they have your name but are missing other details, like your account information or recent activity, it could still be suspicious."

4. Beware of Suspicious Links: "Phishers rely heavily on fake links to trick people," Aarushi continued. "A link might look like it's going to 'instagram.com,' but it actually directs you somewhere completely different. On a computer, you can hover over the link to see where it really leads. On a phone, press and hold the link, but don't click it. If the URL doesn't look right, don't click it."

Kaneera tried it on a few messages in her inbox, quickly noticing that some URLs didn't match what they claimed to be. "It's crazy how easily they can fake these things."

"Yes, and they count on people not checking," Aarushi said. "It's a good habit to always check links before clicking. And if you're unsure, go to the website directly rather than clicking a link from an email or message."

5. Look Out for Poor Grammar and Spelling Errors: "Real companies usually proofread their messages carefully, so if you see obvious spelling or grammar mistakes, it's often a red flag," Aarushi explained. "Phishing emails are often rushed or poorly written, especially if they're coming from overseas."

Kaneera chuckled, recalling a particularly strange message she'd received once. "I remember one that was supposedly from my bank, but it was full of typos. That should've been my first clue."

"Exactly," Aarushi said with a smile. "Mistakes like that are a big warning sign. Most companies take their communication seriously, so if it looks sloppy, be cautious."

6. Check for Unexpected Attachments: "Phishing emails often come with unexpected attachments," Aarushi warned. "They might say it's an invoice, a receipt, or a document you need to review. If you're not expecting an attachment, don't open it. These files often contain malware that can infect your device."

Kaneera was surprised at how common phishing tactics seemed once she knew what to look for. "So I should be careful with any unexpected attachments?"

"Absolutely," Aarushi replied. "If you receive an attachment that seems suspicious, reach out to the person or company directly to confirm before opening it."

7. Verify Any Requests for Personal Information: "A big one to watch for is any message asking for personal or financial information," Aarushi emphasized. "Most companies, especially banks or government agencies, won't ask for sensitive information like passwords, Social Security numbers, or credit card details over email or text. If they do, it's likely a phishing attempt."

Kaneera shook her head, marvelling at how easy it was to overlook these things. "I can't believe I never thought about this before. I've definitely gotten messages like that and didn't even realize they could be phishing attempts."

"Now you'll know," Aarushi said encouragingly. "Whenever you're asked for sensitive info, be extra cautious and try to verify the source."

8. Be Questioning of Unusual Requests from Known Contacts: "Sometimes, phishing messages come from someone you know," Aarushi said, thinking back to Kaneera's experience. "But if they're asking for money, sensitive information, or unusual favors, be cautious. Hackers can sometimes compromise a person's account and send phishing messages to everyone on their contact list."

Kaneera nodded, recalling how her account had been used to send out that suspicious link. "So even if it's from a friend, I should double-check?"

"Exactly, you got it," Aarushi replied. "If you receive a strange message from someone you know, try reaching out to them through another method to confirm. It's better to be safe than sorry."

9. Pay Attention to the Look and Feel of the Message: "Phishing messages often look a little off," Aarushi explained. "The design might not match the company's usual emails, the logo could be blurry, or the formatting might look strange. If something feels different or inconsistent, it could be a phishing attempt."

Kaneera looked through her inbox with a newfound sense of suspicion, noticing small details she'd never paid attention to before. "I can see how easy it is to miss these things, but now that I know what to look for, I feel a lot more confident."

10. When in Doubt, Don't Click or Respond: As Aarushi wrapped up, she offered one last piece of advice. "If you're ever unsure, don't click or respond. It's better to be cautious. Most companies have support teams you can contact to verify the authenticity of a message. And if you're still not sure, just delete it. It's better to lose a few minutes than risk falling for a phishing attempt."

With this new toolkit, Kaneera felt more equipped to handle suspicious messages. She knew what to look for, and for the first time, she felt like she had control over her online security. She thanked Aarushi for breaking it down and is already planning to share this advice with her friends.

Armed with a sharper eye for phishing attempts, Kaneera felt more confident in navigating the digital world safely. But as she'd soon discover, phishing was only one of many tactics hackers could use to invade personal privacy; there were a number of other tactics to which Aarushi herself would become a victim as well. As Aarushi introduced her to the broader range of online threats, Kaneera realized that understanding digital security would be a continuous journey, one where staying informed was key to staying safe.

Chapter 4: Spy in the System

4.1 Aarushi's Laptop Gets Compromised with Spyware

Aarushi noticed something strange on her laptop late one night. She was deep into a research session, looking into laptop settings and online security tools, when her webcam light flickered on for a split second, then went dark. She froze, staring at the tiny light as her mind raced through possible explanations. Had she accidentally clicked a setting? Maybe it was just a harmless glitch?

But deep down, Aarushi knew better. After weeks of helping Kaneera spot suspicious activity on social media and getting Sophia's laptop checked for any lurking threats, she recognized a potential intrusion when she saw one. This wasn't random; something, or someone, was attempting to access her laptop without her permission.

“AARUSHI, YOU OKAY?” Kaneera asked, noticing her sudden silence.

Aarushi took a deep breath, her hands hovering over her keyboard. “I think...someone’s watching me,” she whispered, the weight of her own words sending a chill down her spine. She quickly switched into her techno-savvy mode, immediately launching a scan on her system, her fingers moving rapidly as she searched for anything out of place. It wasn’t long before she found it-a hidden spyware program quietly running in the background, capturing everything she did on her screen.

She looked up at Kaneera and Sophia, both of them watching her with wide, alarmed eyes. “This is serious. Someone installed spyware on my laptop. They’ve been accessing my files, my emails...everything.”

Kaneera’s jaw dropped. “Wait, like... someone could see everything you’ve been doing?”

Aarushi nodded, her voice calm but her mind racing as she calculated the potential damage. “Yes. Spyware like this doesn’t just track what I do online-it can record my keystrokes, access my files, and even turn on my camera. This isn’t just an inconvenience-this is someone invading my privacy in real time.”

Sophia's face darkened, and she clenched her fists, a familiar expression of justice-seeking resolve settling on her face. "This is more than creepy. This is a crime. Whoever's behind this isn't just some troll; they're deliberately targeting us." She was already forming a mental checklist of possible legal actions, her legal instinct kicking in.

Aarushi turned back to her laptop, feeling an unsettling combination of anger and vulnerability as she moved to delete the spyware. But the damage had already been done, and she couldn't help but feel a sense of violation. This wasn't just about data; it was about her personal life, her space, her safety. "We're not just random girls online anymore," she murmured, more to herself than anyone else. "Someone is going out of their way to mess with us."

The three friends sat in silence for a moment, each processing the gravity of the situation. Aarushi could see the worry etched on Kaneera's face and the fierce determination in Sophia's eyes. In their own ways, they were just as shaken as she was.

"I've heard of things like this happening to people," Kaneera said softly, breaking the silence. "But I never thought it would happen to us. I mean, who would want to spy on you?"

"Or why?" Sophia added, her voice stretched with anger. "It's a complete invasion of privacy and security. This isn't just about snooping-it's about control and power." She glanced at Aarushi, silently offering her support.

Aarushi took a deep breath, reminding herself to focus. This was her world-the world of digital threats and intrusions. She had learned from her parents that keeping a cool head was half the battle. "Spyware like this is dangerous because it's so hard to detect. The person behind it could be anywhere, and they could have set this up to track everything I do, every website I visit, every message I send. And we wouldn't even know they're watching." She swallowed hard, feeling the weight of her words.

"So, what do we do now?" Kaneera asked, looking nervously at her own laptop, which she suddenly viewed with suspicion.

Aarushi squared her shoulders, her resolve hardening. "We're going to fight back. First, I'll need to set up stronger protections on all of our devices. We need to assume that if they could get into my laptop, they could be looking at yours, too."

Sophia nodded in agreement, a fierce look in her eyes. "And if we can figure out who's behind this, we can take legal action. This isn't just a digital prank; it's a violation of our rights."

Determined, Aarushi moved quickly, opening her security software and launching a full scan. She began explaining to Kaneera and Sophia how spyware works and why it's such a common tool for cybercriminals. "Spyware isn't just something random hackers use," she explained. "It's used by stalkers, by corporations trying to gather data, and sometimes even by people you know. It's designed to blend in and stay hidden, so you often don't know it's there until it's too late."

She described the dangers, detailing how spyware could track every keystroke she made and turn her camera and microphone on without her knowing. "That's why you'll sometimes see people covering their webcam with a sticker or tape," Aarushi said. "It's a simple precaution, but one that can prevent a lot of trouble."

Kaneera, wide-eyed, quickly picked up a piece of tape and covered her own webcam, prompting a chuckle from Aarushi. "Smart move," she said, offering a small smile despite the tense situation. "It's not a bad idea to do that on any device with a camera."

Aarushi continued, her tone a mix of calm and determination as she set to work, reinforcing her laptop's security. She showed Kaneera and Sophia how to check for unauthorized programs and suspicious activity logs. "Whenever you see something unusual-like a flickering webcam or pop-ups you didn't open-it's worth investigating. Sometimes it's harmless, but other times, like now, it's a sign someone's watching."

Sophia leaned in, her eyes intent. "Is there a way to track them back? To find out who's doing this?"

"It's possible," Aarushi admitted, "but it depends on how skilled they are. Some hackers leave traces, but the ones who know what they're doing can cover their tracks pretty well." She paused, considering their options. "If we can find any evidence, we might be able to trace them back, but it'll take time and precision."

The gravity of the situation settled over them as they sat together, feeling a shared sense of urgency and resolve. For Aarushi, it was a wake-up call-one that reminded her of why she cared so deeply about online safety. For Kaneera, it was a sharp reminder of the risks that came with her open online presence. And for Sophia, it was fuel for her passion for justice, a call to defend herself and her friends in a world that was becoming more digitally hostile.

As the night wore on, they worked together to secure their devices, discussing precautions, tactics, and strategies to keep themselves protected. Aarushi's confidence and knowledge helped reassure them, and though the experience had been unsettling, they felt stronger as a team, knowing they weren't facing it alone.

By the end of the night, Aarushi had made a vow to herself-to dig deeper, to find out who was behind this, and to make sure that no one could so easily invade her life again. This was only the beginning of their journey into the darker side of the digital world, but together, they were ready to take on whatever came next.

4.2 Explanation of Spyware and Malware, How they're installed, and the Dangers

As the initial shock of finding spyware on her laptop began to settle, Aarushi took a deep breath. She needed to explain to Kaneera and Sophia what they were dealing with. Spyware wasn't just a small inconvenience; it was a serious breach that could compromise their privacy, data, and even their safety.

"Okay, so here's the deal," Aarushi began, sitting cross-legged on her bed, her laptop open in front of her. Kaneera and Sophia leaned in, each holding their own devices more cautiously than ever. "Spyware is a type of malware, which is basically any software created to damage, disrupt, or gain unauthorized access to information on a device."

Kaneera looked down at her phone, her eyes wide. "So... malware can just... take over my phone if someone decides they want to?"

"Not exactly," Aarushi replied. "But there are ways it can sneak onto your devices without you even knowing." She looked at her laptop screen, the earlier memory of the webcam flickering still fresh in her mind. "Most spyware is designed to be completely invisible. It operates in the background, silently collecting information-your browsing habits, messages, passwords, even keystrokes."

"Keystrokes?" Sophia asked, her legal mind clicking into gear. "So, it can actually track every key we type?"

Aarushi nodded yes, noticing the look of discomfort on both her friends' faces. "Right. And because spyware can do all of this without showing any visible signs, it's one of the most dangerous types of malware."

1. How Malware and Spyware Sneak In: Kaneera raised her hand like she was back in a classroom. "So, how do people even get this stuff on their devices? I mean, it's not like we're downloading random files or anything."

"That's a good question," Aarushi replied. "Malware can sneak onto your devices in a lot of sneaky ways. Sometimes, it comes bundled with seemingly harmless software or downloads. Other times, it can get in through phishing emails, malicious websites, or infected USB drives."

She continued, "In some cases, spyware and malware are installed when we're tricked into clicking on links that look real but lead to harmful sites. For example, a hacker might send an email pretending to be from your bank, saying there's a problem with your account. You click the link, thinking it's a safe site, but in reality, you're being directed to a fake page that infects your device as soon as you open it."

Sophia's eyes narrowed. "That's deception on another level."

Aarushi nodded. "Exactly. Malware creators rely on people not being cautious or being too trusting. They'll disguise their attacks as links to fun games, discount codes, or even charity organizations. It's all about making people feel safe enough to click without thinking twice."

Kaneera's brows knitted together. "So it's like a trap, designed to look harmless but actually dangerous?"

"Pretty much," Aarushi confirmed. "Once they trick you into letting your guard down, the malware can install itself. And sometimes, it doesn't even need you to click on anything. Just visiting a compromised website can sometimes be enough to let malware in if the site's security is weak."

2. Spyware and Malware in Disguise: "To make it worse," Aarushi went on, "spyware and other malware often come hidden in files that look totally normal. Have you ever received a random file on your email that you weren't expecting, like a document or a photo?"

Sophia nodded, thinking back to the strange email attachments she'd deleted without opening them.

"Well, attackers can make malware look like anything-a document, an image, even a video file. When you open it, it installs in the background, and just like that, it's running on your device."

Kaneera looked horrified. "So, it could be anything? Even a cute cat video?"

Aarushi smiled at Kaneera's reaction, but her tone was serious. "Unfortunately, yes. That's why it's important to only download files and open links from trusted sources. And if you're ever unsure, don't open it. It's better to be safe than to risk infecting your device."

3. The Dangers of Spyware and Malware: Seeing the concern on her friends' faces, Aarushi decided to explain the specific dangers they faced. "Once spyware or malware is installed, it can do a lot of damage. Spyware, for example, can collect information without you even knowing. Every single password you type, every website you visit, and even the messages you send can be captured and sent back to whoever is running the spyware."

Sophia's face darkened. "That's terrifying. This isn't just a tech problem-this is a massive privacy violation."

Aarushi nodded. "Yes. And it's not just about privacy. Some types of malware can do more than just spy on you. Ransomware, for example, locks your files and demands a payment to unlock them. It's like someone breaking into your house, locking all your rooms, and then asking for money before they give you the keys."

Kaneera shook. "Has that ever happened to someone you know?"

Aarushi's expression grew serious. "Unfortunately, yes. Ransomware is one of the most common attacks out there, and it's happened to businesses, hospitals, and even schools. It's not just about locking up data; it disrupts everything. And paying the ransom doesn't always guarantee you'll get your files back."

4. Why Cybercriminals Use Spyware and Malware: "But why would someone do this?" Kaneera asked, genuinely baffled. "What's the point of installing spyware or malware on someone's computer?"

Aarushi took a deep breath. "The motivations vary. Sometimes it's about money. Hackers use spyware to steal personal information, which they can sell on the dark web. They can also use your information to commit fraud, like taking out loans in your name, using your credit card details, or even selling your social media accounts."

Sophia leaned forward. "So, it's like identity theft?"

"Yes, it is," Aarushi said, nodding. "And for some hackers, it's about gaining control. If they have spyware on your device, they can potentially access your camera and your microphone and see what's on your screen. It's a way to manipulate and control people without them ever knowing."

Kaneera shivered. "That's...so creepy. So someone could be watching us, and we wouldn't even know?"

Aarushi gave her friend a sympathetic look. "Yes, that's why it's so important to be aware of the risks. And it's not just strangers. There have been cases where ex-partners, employers, or even friends have installed spyware to monitor someone's activities."

Sophia clenched her fists, and her sense of justice ignited. "This is invasive and wrong on so many levels. There should be stricter laws against this."

5. Protecting against Spyware and Malware: Seeing the concern in her friends' eyes, Aarushi moved on to the practical side. "But the good news is that we can protect ourselves. The first step is awareness, which is what we're doing right now. Recognizing the signs, like unexplained performance issues or strange pop-ups, can be a warning."

Sophia nodded. "And for someone like me, who doesn't know much about tech, what else can I do?"

"There are simple steps," Aarushi reassured her. "First, always have antivirus software installed and keep it updated. Most antivirus programs have a database of known malware, so they can detect and block anything suspicious. Second, avoid downloading attachments or clicking on links from unknown sources."

She continued, "And don't forget to update your software regularly. Companies release updates not just for new features but to patch vulnerabilities that hackers might exploit. By keeping your software up-to-date, you're protecting yourself from many potential threats."

Kaneera looked more confident. "So, it's not just about knowing what to avoid; it's about staying prepared."

Aarushi smiled. "Exactly. By being proactive, you're making it harder for anyone to target you with malware or spyware. And remember to use strong, unique passwords for each of your accounts, so even if one account gets compromised, they can't get into everything."

6. Recognizing the Signs of Malware: Before they wrapped up, Aarushi shared a few warning signs to look out for. "If you ever notice that your device is suddenly slower, or if you see pop-ups you didn't open, that's often a sign of malware. Sometimes, the battery might drain faster than usual, or you might see new programs installed that you didn't download. Those are all red flags."

Kaneera and Sophia listened intently, taking mental notes. They had never thought about these things before, but now they understood just how important it was to stay vigilant.

Aarushi finished, "And finally if you ever suspect something's wrong, run a full scan on your device immediately. It's better to be cautious and catch any issues early than to let them rot."

With a new understanding of the dangers they faced, Kaneera and Sophia were beginning to realize that the digital world they'd always taken for granted was a lot more complex-and a lot more dangerous-than they'd imagined. But they also knew they had a guide in Aarushi, someone who understood the risks and was ready to lead them through the digital maze.

4.3 Strategies for Removing Malware and Securing Devices

After identifying the spyware on her laptop, Aarushi knew she couldn't stop there. If her own system could be infiltrated, it meant any of their devices could be vulnerable. She took a deep breath, turning to Kaneera and Sophia. "Okay, so we've discovered the spyware now, but that's only step one. Now, before going outside, we need to discuss and focus on cleaning it up and securing everything moving forward."

"ISN'T DELETING IT ENOUGH?" Kaneera asked hopefully.

"Not really," Aarushi replied. "Spyware and other types of malware can often hide in your system, sometimes even reinstall themselves after you delete them. We have to be thorough and make sure every trace of it is gone. Here's how we're going to do it."

1. Running a Full System Scan: Aarushi started by explaining the importance of a full system scan. "First, we'll run a full scan using antivirus software. Most good antivirus programs will scan every file and folder on your device, looking for anything suspicious."

Sophia looked intrigued. "Can't we just use the built-in tools?"

"Definitely," Aarushi replied. "For Windows, there's Windows Defender, which is pretty solid for basic protection. MacOS also has built-in protections. But sometimes, additional antivirus software can provide extra layers of security. Look for software that's reputable and regularly updated because new threats are popping up all the time."

She recommended a few reliable options to Kaneera and Sophia. "For a quick scan, the built-in tools can be helpful, but for thorough scanning and monitoring, dedicated antivirus software is usually better, like Bitdefender or Kaspersky antivirus."

2. Booting in Safe Mode: "Sometimes, running a regular scan isn't enough if the malware is too deeply embedded," Aarushi continued. "That's where Safe Mode comes in. Safe Mode loads only the essential parts of your operating system, making it easier to remove stubborn malware."

Kaneera raised her eyebrows. "How do you get into Safe Mode?"

Aarushi smiled, always happy to share a helpful tip. "On Windows, you usually press F8 while booting up, or for newer versions, go to Settings > Update & Security > Recovery and click on 'Restart Now' under Advanced Startup. On a Mac, you just hold down the Shift key when it starts up. Once in Safe Mode, you can run your antivirus scan again, which makes it easier for the software to locate and remove malware that might otherwise be active."

They practiced entering Safe Mode, watching as their systems booted with minimal programs. Aarushi explained, "If there's malware on the system, Safe Mode gives us a better shot at isolating it and deleting it completely."

3. Manually Removing Suspicious Files: After the scan was completed, Aarushi reviewed the results. "If the antivirus didn't catch everything, we might have to get a bit more hands-on and look for suspicious files manually."

Sophia looked hesitant. "How do you know what's suspicious?"

"It can be tricky," Aarushi admitted. "Usually, malware will disguise itself to look like a regular file, but certain red flags can give it away. Files with names that don't make sense, unusually high CPU or memory usage, or files located in unusual folders can sometimes be a sign of malware."

She showed them how to check running processes on their laptops through Task Manager (on Windows) and Activity Monitor (on Mac). "If you see anything that doesn't look right or you're not sure about, it's worth looking it up online before deleting it. Some programs may seem unfamiliar but are essential for your system to run properly, so be careful."

Kaneera took notes, nodding as Aarushi explained the process. "So, we're basically playing detective on our own laptops?"

Aarushi smiled. "Exactly. And if you're ever in doubt, it's better to research a file first rather than deleting something important. But remember, if it's malware, leaving it there can cause more problems."

4. Updating Software and Operating Systems: "One of the easiest ways to secure your device is by keeping everything updated," Aarushi said. "Developers are constantly finding and fixing security flaws. When you don't update, you're leaving open doors for malware to slip through."

Sophia frowned. "But aren't updates annoying? They always seem to pop up at the worst times."

Aarushi chuckled. "I know, but they're essential. Malware developers are always looking for weaknesses in outdated software. By updating regularly, you're closing those vulnerabilities. It's a small inconvenience, but it goes a long way in keeping you safe."

She set up their devices to update automatically, ensuring they'd always have the latest security patches. "Whether it's your operating system, browser, or any other software, keeping them updated will make it harder for malware to get in."

5. Strengthening Account Security with Two-Factor Authentication (2FA): "Another way to secure your devices and accounts is by using two-factor authentication," Aarushi explained. "Even if someone gets your password, 2FA makes it much harder for them to access your account."

Kaneera nodded, intrigued. "How does it work?"

"When you log in, 2FA sends a code to your phone or email," Aarushi explained. "You enter that code to verify it's really you. It's an extra layer of security beyond just a password."

Sophia, with her legal mind, immediately saw the importance. "So, even if someone hacks into our accounts, they'd still need the code?"

"Exactly," Aarushi confirmed. "Without the second factor, they're locked out. And it's not just for social media-bank accounts, email, and other sensitive accounts should all have 2FA enabled if they offer it."

6. Regularly Backing Up Important Data: "Malware, especially ransomware, can result in losing access to all your files," Aarushi explained. "That's why it's crucial to back up your data regularly. If something goes wrong, you'll have copies of everything important."

She recommended two types of backups: cloud storage and external hard drives. "Cloud storage is convenient because it updates automatically, but having an external hard drive backup gives you more control. The key is making sure your backups are secure and that you're not connected to the internet while backing up sensitive data."

Kaneera raised her hand. "So, if my laptop ever gets infected, I can just wipe everything and restore it from a backup?"

Aarushi nodded. "Precisely. Backups give you peace of mind. Even if malware sneaks in, you won't lose anything important."

7. Using Strong, Unique Passwords: "Strong passwords are your first line of defense," Aarushi continued. "Using the same password everywhere is like leaving the same key under the welcome mat for all your doors."

Sophia laughed. "Guilty. I've been using the same password for years."

"Well, it's time to change that," Aarushi replied with a grin. "Passwords should be long, unique, and contain a mix of letters, numbers, and symbols. And avoid using easily guessable information, like birthdays or pet names."

She introduced them to password managers, which can generate and store complex passwords. "It's a way to keep your passwords secure without having to remember them all."

8. Monitoring Device Activity and Permissions: "One thing most people overlook," Aarushi explained, "is checking what permissions apps have on their devices. Malware can sometimes hide in apps that ask for unnecessary permissions, like access to your camera, contacts, or location."

She walked them through their phones and laptops, showing them how to review and manage app permissions. "If an app doesn't need access to something, don't give it. Limiting app permissions keeps you more secure and helps reduce the risk of malware using your information."

Sophia looked thoughtful. "I never thought about that, but it makes sense. I'll check mine tonight."

9. Installing a Firewall: "Firewalls are another great way to protect yourself," Aarushi said. "They act as a barrier between your device and any potential threats online. Most operating systems come with built-in firewalls, but they're not always activated by default."

She showed them how to activate their firewalls and explained how they monitor incoming and outgoing traffic. "Firewalls help prevent unauthorized access to your device, making it harder for hackers or malware to connect to your system."

10. Keeping an Eye on Your Digital Footprint: "Last but not least," Aarushi said, "it's important to be mindful of your online activity. Every website you visit, every app you download, every link you click-it all contributes to your digital footprint."

Kaneera looked puzzled. "And how does that help protect us?"

"The more careful you are, the less chance there is of accidentally inviting malware into your devices," Aarushi explained. "Think of it like being cautious about who you let into your home. If you're selective, you're less likely to let in someone who means harm."

Aarushi leaned back, satisfied with the ground they'd covered. "So, we have a plan for keeping our devices secure. It takes some effort, but it's worth it. The goal is to make your device a fortress that's harder to break into."

Sophia nodded, determination in her eyes. "Thanks, Aarushi. I feel like we actually have some control over this now."

Kaneera smiled. "Yeah, you're like our online security guardian angel."

Aarushi laughed, feeling a surge of pride and relief. She knew that by empowering her friends with this knowledge, she was helping them take back control of their digital lives. And in today's world, that is one of the most valuable skills they could have.

Chapter 5: Passwords and Protection

5.1 Kaneera's Account gets hacked due to Weak Passwords

Kaneera lying on her bed, scrolling through her notifications as usual. She was just about to post a photo from her latest weekend trip when an unexpected email popped up: "Your account password has been changed." Her heart skipped a beat as she stared at the screen. She hadn't changed her password. Panic crept in as she tried logging into her account, only to see the dreaded message: "Password incorrect."

FRUSTRATED, SHE TRIED a few more times, thinking maybe she had mistyped. But the reality soon dawned on her. Someone else had access to her account.

"Um, guys? I think I'm in trouble," Kaneera called out, pacing nervously in her room. Aarushi and Sophia looked up from their own devices, both sensing her anxiety. Aarushi could tell by Kaneera's tone that this wasn't just another minor tech glitch.

"What happened?" Aarushi asked, setting her laptop aside and walking over to Kaneera's phone.

"My Instagram account... I think it's been hacked! Someone changed the password, and I can't get in," Kaneera explained, her voice trembling with a mix of anger and worry. "All my photos, messages, everything-they're just... gone."

Aarushi took Kaneera's phone, her mind racing. "Okay, let's not panic just yet. It sounds like whoever got in might have taken advantage of a weak password."

Kaneera sighed, feeling the sting of frustration. "I know, I know. I didn't think anyone would actually hack me. My password wasn't even that bad! It was 'dancingqueen123'!"

Sophia raised an eyebrow, and Aarushi's mouth quirked in a half-smile. "Kaneera, 'dancingqueen123' is exactly the kind of password hackers love to guess. It's simple, uses common words, and is connected to something personal."

Kaneera groaned. "Fine, it's a little obvious, but I didn't think anyone would actually go after my account."

A Lesson on Password Security

Aarushi explained, "When it comes to passwords, the most important thing is making them strong and hard to guess. Hackers often use something called brute-force attacks, where they try different combinations until they find the right one. Simple passwords make it much easier for them."

"So, what makes a password 'strong'?" Kaneera asked, still feeling the sting of embarrassment.

"Think of it this way," Aarushi began. "A strong password is like a lock with dozens of combinations. Ideally, it should be long, have a mix of uppercase and lowercase letters, numbers, and symbols-and it shouldn't be tied to anything personal, like a favorite song or pet's name."

Kaneera thought about it. "But how am I supposed to remember something like that? I have accounts on everything-social media, email, shopping sites. I can't remember dozens of complex passwords!"

Aarushi nodded sympathetically. "That's where password managers come in. They're like digital safes for your passwords. You only need to remember one strong master password, and the manager stores and generates secure passwords for all your accounts."

Sophia chimed in, "It's actually really convenient once you get used to it. I use one, and I feel so much more secure knowing my passwords are strong and random."

"But what about the people who hacked me?" Kaneera asked, a trace of fear in her voice. "Why would someone go through the trouble of hacking my account?"

Aarushi's expression darkened as she considered the question. "That's what we need to find out. It could be someone just messing around, but it feels... calculated."

She didn't say it aloud, but Aarushi couldn't shake the feeling that someone was watching them, tracking their movements online. This incident didn't feel like a random hacking attempt.

Recovering the Account

Together, they worked to recover Kaneera's account. Aarushi guided her through the account recovery process, helping her verify her identity and regain access. After a few attempts, Kaneera finally received an email confirming that her account had been restored.

"Okay, we're back in," Kaneera breathed a sigh of relief, but Aarushi held up a hand.

"Before you start posting again, let's secure your account properly," she said. "This time, we're creating a stronger password. Something like 'Dq9!Mjw84_x'."

"Are you serious?" Kaneera's eyes widened. "How am I supposed to remember that?"

"You don't have to," Aarushi replied with a grin. "We'll store it in a password manager. That way, you don't have to remember it-it'll be safe and secure."

Aarushi helped Kaneera set up a password manager and explained how it worked. She emphasized the importance of using unique passwords for every account. "If someone hacks one account, they won't automatically have access to everything else," she said.

Adding another Layer of Protection: Two-Factor Authentication

"Another layer of protection you can add is two-factor authentication or 2FA," Aarushi continued. "With 2FA, even if someone gets your password, they won't be able to log in without a second code, usually sent to your phone."

She showed Kaneera how to enable 2FA on her Instagram account and any other accounts she wanted to secure. Kaneera's mood brightened as she realized how much more secure her account was becoming.

"Okay, I'll admit, this is kind of cool," Kaneera said with a smile. "It's like adding an extra lock to my front door."

Aarushi smiled. "Exactly. We're creating a digital fortress around your accounts."

Analyzing the Source of the Attack

After Kaneera's account was fully secured, Aarushi took a step back, her mind whirring with thoughts. This incident felt too personal, too directed. And it wasn't just the weak password that had let someone in-it was as if they had known exactly where to look and when.

"Kaneera, have you noticed anything unusual on your account recently?" Aarushi asked. "Any strange messages, friend requests, or followers?"

Kaneera thought about it. "Actually, there were a couple of weird messages from people I didn't know. They asked for my opinion on some new beauty products, like they were trying to build trust with me. I didn't think much of it, though."

Aarushi's expression grew serious. "This might not be a random hack. Sometimes, hackers will use social engineering tactics to get closer to their targets. They'll try to interact with you to learn more about you and find vulnerabilities. It's not just about the password-it's about gathering as much information as possible."

Sophia, who had been listening closely, spoke up. "So, you're saying someone might have been studying Kaneera's account, figuring out her habits?"

"Exactly," Aarushi replied. "They could have been waiting for the perfect moment to strike. And since your password was easy to guess, it made it that much easier for them."

Kaneera shuddered at the thought. "That's so creepy. Do you think it could be... the same person who's been causing all the other issues?"

Aarushi hesitated, not wanting to worry her friends unnecessarily. "It's possible. But either way, this just shows how important it is to stay vigilant. We have to assume that anyone online could be watching or trying to gather information."

A Lesson Learned

As they finished securing Kaneera's account, Aarushi took a moment to reflect. They had managed to fix the immediate issue, but it was clear that they were dealing with more than just minor inconveniences. Someone was watching them, tracking their digital footprints, and waiting for opportunities to exploit their vulnerabilities.

"Aarushi, thank you," Kaneera said, her voice tinged with gratitude. "I would have been lost without your help."

"Don't mention it," Aarushi replied with a reassuring smile. "Just remember, in the digital world, passwords are like the keys to your home. You wouldn't leave your front door unlocked, right?"

Kaneera laughed. "Lesson learned. From now on, I'm making my digital doors as secure as possible."

A Lasting Question

As they closed out the session, Aarushi couldn't shake the sense that they were missing something-something important. Who was behind all these attacks? And what were they after? It was only a matter of time before they uncovered the truth, but for now, they'd take each incident as a lesson, readying their defenses and staying one step ahead.

And with that, they moved forward, knowing that every step brought them closer to facing the elusive figure behind it all.

5.2 The Importance of Strong Passwords, Password Managers, and Two-Factor Authentication

As the trio sat back after securing Kaneera's account, Aarushi couldn't help but feel this was the perfect moment to emphasize the importance of a solid digital defense. In an age where passwords are like the keys to one's entire online life, it was essential to make sure they were up to the task.

"Okay, Kaneera," Aarushi started, taking a deep breath. "Now that we've saved your account from the brink of disaster let's talk about what makes a good password-and why it's more important than ever to keep it secure."

Kaneera nodded, feeling both chastised and intrigued. "I get it. 'Dancingqueen123' probably wasn't the best choice."

Sophia gave her a sympathetic smile. "Hey, we've all been there. I used to use my pet's name for every single account until Aarushi talked some sense into me."

Aarushi laughed. "Exactly. Let's discuss why strong passwords matter, how we can make them stronger, and the tools that make this all manageable."

The Anatomy of a Strong Password

Aarushi pulled out her laptop and typed in a few examples for Kaneera and Sophia to see. "A strong password is like a solid lock on a door. It has to be complex enough to withstand attempts to break in. But what does that mean in the digital world?"

She pointed to the screen. "A strong password usually meets these criteria:

- Length: At least 12 characters, ideally longer.
- Complexity: A mix of uppercase and lowercase letters, numbers, and symbols.
- Unpredictability: Avoids common words, phrases, or anything related to personal information-like birthdays or favourite songs."

She gave Kaneera a playful smirk. "See, no more 'dancingqueen' passwords!"

Sophia looked thoughtful. "It sounds like these passwords are supposed to be hard to guess but also hard to remember. How are we supposed to keep track of all that?"

"That's where password managers come in," Aarushi said with a grin.

The Lifesaver: Password Managers

Kaneera raised an eyebrow as Aarushi opened her password manager and displayed a list of securely stored passwords. "So, instead of remembering dozens of different passwords, you just need to remember one strong master password for your password manager."

"What's a password manager, exactly?" Kaneera asked, leaning in with curiosity.

Aarushi explained, "It's a secure tool that stores all your passwords in an encrypted vault. Whenever you need to log into a site, you just open the password manager, and it auto-fills the password for you. That way, you can have a unique, complex password for each account without memorizing them all."

Sophia nodded, looking impressed. "So, you're saying even if one password gets hacked, the others are safe because they're all different?"

"Exactly," Aarushi replied. "Password managers help keep things organized and secure, especially if you're like most people with accounts on dozens of sites."

Kaneera considered it. "But what if someone hacks into the password manager itself? Wouldn't they have access to everything?"

Aarushi smiled, having anticipated this question. "Good point. Password managers use encryption, so even if someone got into your account, they wouldn't be able to read the passwords without the master password. Plus, many password managers also support two-factor authentication for an added layer of security."

Sophia chimed in, "So, basically, a password manager is like having a digital vault, with each account having its own unique lock."

"Exactly," Aarushi confirmed. "And when it comes to digital security, that's invaluable."

Why Reusing Passwords Is a Major Risk

Aarushi took a moment to stress the importance of using unique passwords for each account. "Let's say you use the same password on your social media, email, and bank accounts," she explained. "If a hacker cracks it on one site, they now have access to everything. This is called a credential stuffing attack-hackers try the same password across multiple sites, hoping it works elsewhere."

Kaneera shuddered. "So just one mistake could lead to everything getting hacked?"

Aarushi nodded. "That's why unique passwords are so essential. Even if one account gets compromised, the damage stops there."

Adding Extra Security with Two-Factor Authentication (2FA)

Aarushi leaned forward, a serious expression on her face. "There's one more thing we need to talk about, and it's called two-factor authentication, or 2FA. Think of it as adding a second lock to your door. Even if someone has your password, they still need the second 'key' to get in."

Kaneera looked intrigued. "How does that work?"

"Whenever you log in, you'll enter your password as usual," Aarushi explained. "But before you can access your account, you'll have to provide a second piece of information. This is usually a code sent to your phone or generated by an app. It's a way to double-check that it's really you logging in."

Sophia chimed in, "So even if a hacker has my password, they won't be able to log in without my phone?"

"Exactly," Aarushi replied. "2FA makes it significantly harder for hackers to get into your account, even if they have your password. It's like having an extra layer of security, and it's one of the best ways to protect your accounts."

Real-Life Example: How 2FA could've Prevented Kaneera's Hack

Kaneera raised her hand in a mock surrender. "Okay, okay, I get it. But are you saying that 2FA could have stopped my account from getting hacked?"

Aarushi nodded. "If you had 2FA enabled, the hacker would have needed both your password and your phone to log in. Even if they guessed 'dancingqueen123,' they wouldn't have been able to get past the second step."

Sophia grinned. "Kaneera looks like 2FA would have saved your dance photos."

Kaneera laughed, but her expression turned serious. "I feel like I got off easy this time, but I don't want to take any more chances."

Aarushi nodded approvingly. "That's the mindset you need. 2FA isn't perfect, but it makes things significantly harder for anyone trying to break into your account."

Setting Up 2FA and a Strong Master Password

Aarushi spent the next few minutes helping Kaneera set up 2FA on her most important accounts, like email and social media. She also guided her through choosing a strong master password for her password manager. After a few tries, they settled on a password that felt secure and memorable.

"It's a bit long, but I'll get used to it," Kaneera said, giving Aarushi a grateful smile. "And knowing its keeping my accounts safe is totally worth it."

A New Approach to Online Security

As they wrapped up, Aarushi took a moment to reflect. "Here's the thing, guys. Strong passwords, password managers, and 2FA are like the basics of online security. They're not just things to check off a list-they're habits that protect you."

Sophia nodded thoughtfully. "It's like building good habits with money or health. It might seem small, but it makes a huge difference in the long run."

"Exactly," Aarushi replied. "Hackers rely on people being careless with passwords. By taking these extra steps, you're making it much harder for anyone to mess with you."

A Mysterious Reminder

Just as they finished up, Kaneera's phone vibrated. She checked it, her face going pale. "I just got a message from an unknown number. It says, 'Nice try, but we'll be back.'"

Sophia and Aarushi looked at each other, their expressions mirroring Kaneera's unease. This wasn't just a random hack-someone was clearly targeting them. But why?

Aarushi felt a chill run down her spine. The message was a warning, a taunt, and a promise all at once. Whoever was behind this attack wasn't finished. But as unsettling as it was, Aarushi felt a renewed determination. They'd fortified their defenses, and they were ready for whatever came next.

"Alright," she said, her voice steady. "Let's keep our guard up. This won't be the last we hear from them, but we're prepared."

With their accounts secure and their minds focused, the trio braced for the next challenge. They knew their journey into online security wasn't over-in fact, it was just beginning.

5.3 How they Recover the Account and secure their Personal Data

The mystery message had sent a chill through the group, but it had also sparked a newfound determination in each of them. Aarushi took charge, her mind immediately jumping to the best methods for recovering Kaneera's account and fortifying their digital lives.

"Okay, Kaneera," Aarushi said, her voice calm and reassuring. "First, we need to regain control of your account. Once we're in, we'll set things up so this can't happen again."

Kaneera nodded, though her hands were trembling slightly. "I'm ready. Let's do this."

Step 1: Regaining Control

Aarushi opened her laptop and guided Kaneera through the initial steps. "First things first: let's see if you can still access your account using 'forgot password.' This should help if they haven't changed the recovery email."

Kaneera clicked on the "forgot password" link and entered her email. Thankfully, the system prompted her to verify her identity by sending a recovery code to her email.

"Check your inbox, Kaneera," Aarushi instructed, her eyes steady. "If you get that code, we'll know they haven't fully taken over."

Kaneera opened her email on her phone, and relief washed over her face when the recovery code arrived. "Got it!" she exclaimed, typing in the code and resetting her password.

"Good," Aarushi said, smiling. "Now, choose a strong password that's nothing like your previous one."

Kaneera laughed nervously, entering a new, complex password with Aarushi's help. She added symbols, numbers, and a mix of letters, feeling more secure with each character she typed.

Step 2: Checking for Suspicious Activity

"Now that we're back in, let's go over the account's recent activity," Aarushi advised. "We need to make sure they haven't done anything else while they had control."

They navigated to the activity log and scrolled through Kaneera's recent logins and messages. Several unfamiliar logins caught their eye, originating from locations Kaneera had never been to.

"They were accessing it from all over," Kaneera said, her face pale. "This feels invasive."

Sophia placed a comforting hand on Kaneera's shoulder. "It is, but we're taking the right steps to make sure this doesn't happen again."

Aarushi chimed in, "Exactly. And look here-nothing else seems changed. That's a good sign. We'll log out of all devices to ensure they're completely locked out."

They selected the option to "log out of all devices," which immediately severed any open sessions on other computers or phones. Kaneera exhaled, visibly relieved.

Step 3: Strengthening Security with 2FA and a Password Manager

"Now, let's add two-factor authentication to this account," Aarushi continued, navigating to Kaneera's account security settings. "That way, even if someone gets your password, they'll need access to your phone to log in."

They activated 2FA, and Kaneera received a verification code on her phone as part of the setup process. Once it was enabled, Aarushi added, "Now, even if someone tries to break in, they'll be blocked unless they have that second code."

Sophia nodded approvingly. "This makes me want to secure all my accounts with 2FA."

"That's a good idea," Aarushi agreed. "We should all take a few minutes to secure our main accounts the same way. And let's use the password manager we talked about. It'll keep track of all your complex passwords without you needing to memorize them."

Aarushi helped both Kaneera and Sophia install a password manager, guiding them through the setup. With each password they saved, Kaneera felt an extra layer of security building around her digital life.

Step 4: Reviewing Connected Apps and Permissions

"Next up," Aarushi said, "let's check the apps and devices connected to your account. Sometimes, attackers add apps to monitor or control your account even after you've changed your password."

They went to the "connected apps" section of Kaneera's account and found two unfamiliar apps that had been granted access. Aarushi explained, "These apps can be used to control accounts remotely or gather information."

They removed the suspicious apps, ensuring they couldn't re-establish control over Kaneera's account.

Step 5: Securing Other Accounts and Information

With Kaneera's social media account back under her control, Aarushi suggested they review security on all accounts tied to Kaneera's email. "Sometimes, hackers target emails, bank accounts, or other important services after gaining access to one account."

The group worked together to ensure Kaneera's email and other critical accounts were secure with updated passwords and 2FA. Aarushi also suggested checking for any recent changes in these accounts to confirm they hadn't been compromised.

Kaneera sighed with relief, feeling safer with each account they updated. "I never realized how much was connected until now," she admitted.

"It's all about being proactive," Aarushi reassured her. "Now that we've locked things down let's look into securing your personal data."

Step 6: Personal Data and Privacy Settings

They began adjusting Kaneera's privacy settings, ensuring her posts, photos, and personal information were only visible to close friends. Aarushi explained, "Oversharing can make you vulnerable to identity theft or other risks, so let's make sure your details are private."

Kaneera nodded, grateful for the guidance. They adjusted her privacy settings, removing any personal information that didn't need to be public and reducing visibility for her contact details.

Sophia chimed in, "Maybe this is something we should all look into. Privacy settings can keep a lot of unwanted attention away."

Aarushi smiled. "Absolutely. The less information that's available for strangers to see, the less power anyone has to use it against you."

Step 7: Monitoring for Future Threats

Finally, Aarushi suggested setting up alerts for unusual activity. "Most platforms have options to notify you if there's suspicious activity on your account. Let's set that up so you get alerts if someone tries to log in from an unfamiliar device or location."

Kaneera activated alerts on her social media and email accounts, giving her an early warning system if her account was ever at risk again.

With a sense of accomplishment, they completed their checklist. Kaneera's account was fortified, her information was secured, and her settings were optimized for privacy.

Reflecting on Lessons Learned

Kaneera leaned back, visibly more at ease. "I feel like I've taken my digital security for granted for too long."

Aarushi nodded, her expression serious but kind. "We all do at some point. The key is to learn from it and make sure we're protected going forward."

Sophia added, "It's a reminder for all of us. We live so much of our lives online, and we need to treat our digital security like we treat physical security."

As they wrapped up, a new notification popped up on Kaneera's phone. It was a message from the same unknown number: "Think you're safe now? You're just getting started."

The message was a cold reminder that, even with all their newfound precautions, the shadow lurking behind the scenes wasn't ready to back down. The words left them shaken but even more resolved to stay vigilant.

Aarushi closed her laptop, her mind whirling with the next steps they needed to take. This wasn't just about one hacked account or one close call. It was about staying one step ahead and building a defense that could withstand even the most relentless attacks.

Chapter 6: Cyberstalker Unmasked

6.1 The Cyberstalker Escalates, Leading to Doxxing and Threats

Aarushi sensed it first. She had a gnawing feeling in her gut that their online troubles were far from over. Kaneera's account hack had been a close call, and the trio had learned a lot, but things were about to get far more personal.

It started with an innocuous post on Kaneera's feed-a selfie taken at a popular café. "#MorningVibes #CityLife," she had captioned it, her favorite coffee cup and pastry in hand. It seemed harmless enough, a typical share for Kaneera's followers who adored her lifestyle posts. But later that evening, as they were celebrating Kaneera's restored account with a quiet get-together at Sophia's place, her phone pinged with an alarming notification.

She glanced at it, expecting another like or comment, but her face went pale. “Uh, guys?” she whispered, her voice barely audible as she held up her phone. A stranger had commented, “Hope you enjoyed that croissant at Parker Street Café… you’ll be seeing us soon.”

The message, disturbingly precise and too specific to be ignored, sent a chill down Aarushi’s spine. “Wait,” Sophia said, frowning as she scanned the post, “How do they know exactly where you were?”

Aarushi’s expression turned grim. “This isn’t just someone leaving a creepy comment. This is targeted. They’re tracking your real-time location.”

Kaneera sat frozen, her hands gripping her phone tightly. “Is this… normal? Can people just… know where I am like this?”

The Escalation Begins

Aarushi took a deep breath, trying to stay calm for her friend. “It’s not normal, but it can happen if someone is really trying to track you. Based on what we know, this could mean they’ve been watching your posts for patterns or maybe even compromised your device.”

But it wasn’t until a few hours later, when another notification popped up on Kaneera’s phone, that the seriousness of the situation became undeniable. This time, the message wasn’t from a random user. It was a direct message containing an image-a grainy photo of Kaneera and Sophia from that afternoon, sitting together in the café. The caption read, “We’re closer than you think.”

Sophia’s face blanched as she looked at the picture. “This isn’t just a game,” she muttered, her voice shaking with anger. “This is stalking.”

The situation escalated rapidly after that. Aarushi, now on high alert, spent hours combing through Kaneera’s account for anything unusual, but nothing stood out. Whoever this person was, they were careful-meticulous even, about covering their tracks.

And then, the unthinkable happened.

The Doxxing Threat

A few days later, Kaneera’s phone started buzzing with an influx of texts, emails and even calls from strangers. Her social media accounts were suddenly flooded with aggressive comments, calling her names and threatening her. “What’s going on?” she cried out, her voice shaky with fear as her phone seemed to buzz non-stop.

Aarushi and Sophia rushed over to her, each trying to make sense of the chaos. "Let me see," Aarushi demanded, her voice firm and steady. She took Kaneera's phone, scrolling through the flood of messages and comments.

Her eyes widened as she saw a public post from a dummy account with Kaneera's name, phone number, and even her home address. This wasn't just harassment-it was doxxing, a terrifying invasion of privacy where someone's personal information is leaked online for malicious purposes. Kaneera's private life was now on full display for everyone to see.

"This is serious," Aarushi said, her voice a mix of anger and concern. "Whoever's doing this wants you to feel threatened and exposed. This is an escalation, and we need to act fast."

Sophia nodded, determined. "This isn't just a random act anymore. This is someone deliberately trying to intimidate you."

Understanding the Motive

As they discussed the situation, Aarushi's mind raced, piecing together the cyberstalker's motivations. "Kaneera, think back. Have you had any confrontations online? Anyone who might hold a grudge?"

Kaneera thought hard, then shook her head. "Nothing serious... just some trolls, but I've blocked them. I never thought anyone would actually come after me like this."

Sophia interjected her legal mind at work. "Stalking and doxxing aren't just creepy; they're illegal. This could be someone who feels like you wronged them, but this level of escalation usually comes from someone with a personal vendetta."

Aarushi nodded, knowing that whoever was targeting Kaneera wasn't just trying to scare her-they wanted control. The idea of a stalker lurking in the background, watching every move, tracking every location, and leaking personal information was beyond unsettling.

"We have to report this," Aarushi said, meeting their worried faces with determination. "If they're willing to leak personal details, who knows what they're planning next?"

Action Plan: Securing Kaneera's Information

First, they reported the post containing Kaneera's information to the social media platform, flagging it as a severe privacy violation. Aarushi guided Kaneera through contacting customer support, requesting an urgent review to have the doxxing post taken down. They contacted the phone carrier to temporarily change Kaneera's number and ensured that she updated her privacy settings across all social media platforms.

"Let's go through each of your accounts," Aarushi suggested, carefully checking Kaneera's privacy settings to ensure nothing was visible to anyone outside her trusted circle.

But Aarushi knew these measures alone wouldn't be enough. "This person clearly has some access to your personal data," she explained. "If they're this dedicated, we need to dig deeper into where they might be getting your information."

Aarushi recommended Kaneera remove geotags from any past posts and avoid real-time location sharing entirely. They went over every app, disabling location services, restricting permissions, and deleting any unnecessary apps.

"Also," Aarushi added, "be cautious about any online forms or sites you use. Hackers sometimes find information through simple online interactions, and you'd be surprised how much people give away."

Building a Defense Strategy

After a long night of working on Kaneera's digital security, they took a break, sitting in silence as the weight of the situation set in. But Aarushi, as always, was determined to find answers.

"Listen," she said gently, "I know this is overwhelming. But we're going to beat this. We'll make sure every possible vulnerability is closed. And together, we'll figure out who's behind this."

Kaneera nodded, though tears welled in her eyes. "I just don't understand why anyone would do this. I didn't even think it was possible for someone to find so much about me."

Sophia leaned forward, her expression firm. "People like this cyberstalker thrive on fear and power. They rely on us feeling helpless, but we're not. We're learning how to fight back."

The conversation shifted to their own experiences with privacy and security. Kaneera reflected on how easy it was to share details without considering the risks, while Aarushi explained the importance of controlled sharing.

As they talked, Aarushi noticed a shift in Kaneera's outlook-a determination growing from within. "I'm done being a victim," Kaneera whispered, wiping away her tears. "I want to understand how to protect myself."

A New Resolve

Aarushi's face softened. "That's the spirit. And we're here to make sure this doesn't happen again."

That night, they took their first real steps in creating a digital security plan. Aarushi walked them through best practices for handling threats like doxxing and stalking, sharing the strategies she knew would make a difference. They added trusted contacts to Kaneera's emergency contacts list and discussed setting up a VPN to mask her IP address when browsing.

Sophia added, "And legally, we're in the right. I'll start researching ways we can document all this evidence. If this escalates further, we'll have a case."

As they wrapped up, a notification lit up Aarushi's screen. It was an email from an unfamiliar address, with the subject line: "You can't hide."

She clicked it open, her heart pounding. Inside was a single line: "I see you've been busy."

Aarushi closed the laptop, her face resolute. This was no longer about securing a social media account or removing spyware. This was personal, and it was only the beginning of their journey into the dark underbelly of online menaces.

The girls glanced at each other, a mix of fear and fierce determination in their eyes. They weren't just reacting to threats anymore-they were preparing to fight back, to unmask the stalker, and to reclaim their peace of mind.

Little did they know, this was only the start of their journey into a world where digital security wasn't just about protecting data; it was about protecting themselves, their identities, and the very lives they led online and off.

6.2 Understanding Cyberstalking, Doxxing, and the Impact on Privacy

Aarushi leaned back, rubbing her eyes as she scanned through the information she had pulled up on her laptop. The more she researched cyberstalking and doxxing, the clearer it became that what Kaneera was experiencing was no small matter. It wasn't just about some stranger snooping around-it was a violation of Kaneera's right to privacy and safety.

Gathered in Sophia's cozy apartment, the three friends huddled around Aarushi's laptop, their faces illuminated by the screen's glow. The air felt heavy with tension, and each of them knew they were facing a real threat, not just an annoying online troll. Aarushi clicked on a news article detailing a recent case of doxxing, and Kaneera winced as she read the headline aloud: "Influencer's Address Leaked, Forced to Move Amidst Online Harassment."

Sophia broke the silence. "I knew that cyberstalking was a thing, but I didn't realize how serious it could get." She shook her head, the reality sinking in. "It's like someone is turning your entire life into their playground."

Aarushi nodded. "Yes. Cyberstalking and doxxing aren't just online hassles; they're direct attacks on someone's privacy. And in our digital world, that privacy is often the only thing keeping us safe."

The Anatomy of Cyberstalking

Aarushi explained, "Cyberstalking is when someone uses the internet to harass, monitor, or intimidate another person. It's like regular stalking, but it's done from behind a screen, which often makes it easier for them to hide."

Kaneera was surprised, realizing how closely this definition mirrored her own experience. "But why would anyone do this?" she asked, her voice a mix of fear and disbelief.

"There are a lot of reasons," Aarushi replied thoughtfully. "Sometimes it's personal, like an ex or someone who holds a grudge. But other times, it's about power and control. A cyberstalker can watch someone's every move, learn their routines, and manipulate them without ever being in the same room. It's chilling because the stalker is always just out of reach."

Sophia chimed in. "And unlike traditional stalking, which might be limited by physical proximity, cyberstalking can happen from anywhere in the world. The person could be right down the street, or they could be halfway across the globe. The anonymity of the internet makes it even harder to catch them."

Aarushi nodded, continuing, "Cyberstalkers can use a range of tactics to monitor or harass their targets. It starts with something as simple as following their social media profiles and analyzing each post, photo, and comment. But it can escalate to more invasive tactics, like tracking someone's location, digging through personal information, and even hacking into accounts."

Kaneera while being angry. "So it's not just about what I post publicly, then?"

"No," Aarushi replied. "Cyberstalkers can use social engineering tricks, like pretending to be someone else, to gain access to private information. They might find out where you work, your favorite hangouts, or even details about your friends and family. Once they have that, it's like they have a map of your life."

Doxxing: A More Aggressive Threat

Sophia looked serious as she added, "And that's where doxxing comes in. Doxxing is one of the most invasive tactics a cyberstalker can use. It's when someone publicly shares your private information, like your address, phone number, or even your workplace, with malicious intent."

Kaneera's face paled. "So it's like giving my personal information to strangers?"

"Yes," Aarushi said grimly. "And the worst part is that once it's out there, it's nearly impossible to get it back. That information gets reposted, shared across forums, and even spread through social media. It only takes one person to make your life a living nightmare."

Sophia scrolled through a few legal articles she had found. "The scary part is that doxxing can lead to real-world consequences. People who get doxxed often face harassment from strangers, even in their own neighborhoods. Some have to move, change their numbers, or go into hiding."

Kaneera shivered, realizing how close she had come to facing such a fate. "So, it's not just about feeling uncomfortable-it's actually dangerous."

"Exactly," Aarushi replied. "Doxxing isn't just a digital attack; it's a threat to physical safety. Once your personal information is out there, it gives anyone with ill intentions easy access to you. You could be getting threatening calls, unwanted visitors, and there's always the risk of escalation."

The Psychological Impact of Cyberstalking and Doxxing

Aarushi paused, looking at Kaneera and Sophia. "It's easy to think of cyberstalking and doxxing as just online issues, but they're much more than that. They can deeply impact someone's mental health."

Sophia nodded. "Imagine feeling like you're constantly being watched. You start second-guessing every post, wondering who's seeing it and what they're doing with that information."

Kaneera's expression softened, a new layer of understanding settling in. "It's exhausting. I already feel paranoid just from these last few incidents. It's like I can't even relax in my own space anymore."

"That's exactly what these attackers want," Aarushi said, her tone serious. "Cyberstalking and doxxing are meant to make you feel vulnerable, to strip away your sense of security. Victims often develop anxiety, depression, and even paranoia. They might withdraw from social activities, stop posting online, or feel like they're constantly being watched."

Sophia added, "And it doesn't just end when the harassment stops. Even after the stalker is gone, the fear can stay with someone. They might feel the need to be extra cautious, sometimes for years, because the trust they once had in their own privacy has been shattered."

Aarushi sighed. "The problem is, many people don't take these threats seriously until it happens to them. It's so easy to think, 'That'll never happen to me,' but the truth is, and anyone with an online presence is at risk."

Why Digital Privacy is Critical

"Online privacy is more important than ever because of exactly these kinds of threats," Aarushi explained. "When we're online, we're sharing parts of ourselves-our interests, our location, our routines. That information can be pieced together like a puzzle. It gives strangers insights into our lives that we might not even be aware of."

Sophia crossed her arms thoughtfully. "And once someone knows enough about you, they can manipulate you. It could be something as small as guessing your security questions or as severe as threatening your safety."

Kaneera nodded slowly, her face serious. "I used to think that my posts were just harmless, but now I see how even the smallest details can reveal a lot."

Aarushi continued, "It's not about being paranoid. It's about being aware of how much we're sharing and who might be watching. The internet is vast, and just because we're behind a screen doesn't mean we're safe from harm."

Defensive Measures against Cyberstalking and Doxxing

Sophia leaned forward, interested. "So what can people do to protect themselves?"

"Firstly, be cautious about what you post online," Aarushi advised. "Avoid sharing real-time locations, and think twice about what personal details you're revealing. Even something as simple as a favorite café can give away a pattern."

Sophia nodded, scribbling notes. "Makes sense. It's about limiting the breadcrumbs that lead back to us."

"Exactly," Aarushi replied. "Another essential step is securing all of your accounts. Use strong, unique passwords and two-factor authentication, and avoid oversharing personal details, even in private chats. Cyberstalkers can find ways to infiltrate seemingly harmless spaces."

Kaneera asked, "But what about when information is already out there?"

"In cases where your information is already public, consider taking down any unnecessary posts or requesting to remove outdated information from search engines. You can also reach out to platforms for help in removing personal data, though it's a bit of a process," Aarushi explained.

Sophia added, "And from a legal perspective, document everything. Save screenshots, emails, and messages. In case this escalates, it's essential to have evidence."

Aarushi nodded. "Good point, Sophia. Keeping records not only helps you prove your case but also gives you something tangible to present to authorities if it ever reaches that point."

A SHIFT IN PERSPECTIVE

Kaneera sat quietly, absorbing the weight of their conversation. For years, she had loved the freedom of sharing her life online, never questioning the potential risks. But now, she saw that the digital world held more dangers than she had realized.

"Maybe I should just stop posting altogether," she whispered, the fear evident in her voice.

Aarushi placed a comforting hand on her shoulder. "It's not about quitting, Kaneera. It's about being informed and taking control. You can still share your life, but in a way that protects your privacy.

It's all about balance."

Sophia agreed, her tone supportive. "We just have to be smarter about it. Knowing how to protect ourselves gives us the power to keep doing what we love without feeling vulnerable."

Kaneera looked between her friends, the worry in her eyes fading slightly. "You're right. I don't want this person, whoever they are, to take away the things I enjoy. I just need to be more careful."

Aarushi smiled. “Exactly. And we’re all learning together. Every step we take makes us stronger, and the more we know, the harder it is for anyone to use the internet against us.”

With a renewed resolve, the three friends knew they weren’t just protecting themselves; they were arming themselves with the knowledge to confront anyone who dared threaten their privacy. But as they would soon discover, awareness alone wouldn’t be enough to keep the stalker at bay. In a world where digital shadows lurked at every corner, they would need every skill and strategy Aarushi could teach them.

6.3 Strategies for Dealing with Stalkers and Securing Private Information

The atmosphere in Sophia's apartment was heavy as Aarushi, Kaneera, and Sophia sat down to discuss what they could do about Kaneera's stalker. The incidents had escalated, and their experiences had left each of them with a lingering sense of vulnerability. But despite the fear, Aarushi was determined to find a way to protect her friends. She had spent hours researching different tactics and strategies to ward off potential stalkers and secure their digital lives, and now, she was ready to share what she had learned.

"First things first," Aarushi began, pulling up a series of steps on her laptop. "We need to create a system that keeps us safe and helps prevent situations like this from happening again. I'll walk us through the most effective strategies for dealing with online threats and securing our private information."

Kaneera and Sophia leaned forward, listening intently as Aarushi laid out her plan.

Understanding Boundaries: Identifying and Blocking Threats

"One of the first things to remember," Aarushi explained, "is to recognize when someone's behavior crosses a line. It's easy to ignore unusual interactions online, but the moment someone seems overly intrusive or begins monitoring your activities, it's time to set boundaries."

Sophia nodded thoughtfully. "So, it's not just about ignoring comments or messages?"

"Right," Aarushi replied. "If someone's repeatedly showing up in your life-whether it's by leaving comments, sending messages, or liking every post you make-it's essential to keep an eye on them. This can be an early sign of someone who might escalate their behavior."

Aarushi clicked on a tab to show examples of red flags to watch for, such as repetitive interactions, unsolicited messages, and over-familiarity with strangers. "When in doubt, don't hesitate to use the block feature. Most platforms make it easy to block users who are acting suspiciously."

"Blocking isn't rude," Kaneera chimed in, almost as if convincing herself. "It's a form of self-protection."

Adjusting Privacy Settings for Enhanced Security

Aarushi opened a social media app and navigated to the privacy settings menu. "Privacy settings are often underestimated, but they're essential for keeping your information secure. We should be using the highest privacy settings available."

She continued, "Start by limiting who can see your posts. Change your profile visibility to 'Friends Only' or 'Followers Only,' and avoid making information like your email, phone number, or address visible. Make sure only trusted people have access to your content."

Sophia leaned in. "And what about our location? Should we stop tagging it altogether?"

"Yes," Aarushi confirmed. "Turning off location tagging and restricting who can see your location is crucial. For places you frequent, like your home, gym, or favorite café, avoid tagging yourself there in real-time. If you want to share where you've been, do it after you've left. This minimizes the chances of someone tracking your movements."

Kaneera made a note on her phone. "From now on, I'll be more mindful about what I share, especially about my location."

Using Strong, Unique Passwords and Two-Factor Authentication

"Passwords are one of the most straightforward yet powerful tools we have for protecting ourselves," Aarushi said, emphasizing the importance of using strong, unique passwords for every account. "If your accounts share the same password and one of them is compromised, the others are at risk."

Sophia added, "I know we talked about passwords before, but could you remind us of some best practices?"

"Of course," Aarushi replied. "Use at least 12 characters, including letters, numbers, and symbols. Avoid using obvious things like your name, birthday, or simple phrases. And please, never use 'password123'!"

The girls laughed, easing the tension.

Aarushi continued, "Two-factor authentication, or 2FA, is another must. It's an added layer of security where you'll need to enter a code sent to your phone or email after you input your password. This way, even if someone manages to steal your password, they'll have a hard time accessing your account."

Kaneera looked relieved. "I'll set up 2FA on all my accounts tonight."

Avoiding Phishing and Social Engineering Traps

Sophia, always the critical thinker, asked, "But what if someone tries to trick us into giving them our information? You know, like those phishing schemes?"

Aarushi nodded. "Phishing and social engineering are common tactics for gathering personal information. Always be cautious when you receive an unsolicited message, email, or link. If you're not sure about a message's authenticity, don't respond to it and never click on unknown links."

Kaneera chimed in, "And if it looks like it's from a friend?"

"Even then," Aarushi replied, "it's wise to double-check. Hackers can make messages look like they're from someone you know. Always verify with the person directly through another method, like calling or texting, before you trust anything that seems suspicious."

Creating a Digital Paper Trail

Sophia, ever the budding legal professional, asked, "What about proof? In case things go further?"

Aarushi turned to her with a smile. "That's a great point. Creating a digital paper trail is crucial. Document every incident, no matter how small. Take screenshots of messages, emails, and any suspicious interactions. Having a record makes it easier to show evidence if you need to report someone."

Sophia nodded approvingly, taking notes. "This will definitely come in handy if we ever need to file a report."

Securing Devices with Anti-Malware Tools

"One major aspect of protecting our information is ensuring our devices are secure," Aarushi said, opening a tab to demonstrate a few recommended anti-malware programs. "Using antivirus and anti-malware software is essential. This software can detect and remove any malicious programs before they can do damage."

Sophia asked, "And this includes spyware, right?"

"Yes, absolutely," Aarushi confirmed. "High-quality anti-malware software can catch spyware, keyloggers, and other harmful software. Just make sure to keep it updated and schedule regular scans."

Limiting Personal Information on Public Profiles

Aarushi explained how limiting what they shared online could prevent potential stalkers from gathering details. "One of the biggest mistakes people make is sharing too much. Avoid sharing personal information on public profiles. For instance, don't include your birthday, address, or even specific interests that might make it easy for someone to figure out your location or routine."

Kaneera reflected, "I never realized how many details about myself I was putting out there without even thinking about it."

Aarushi nodded. "It's a common mistake. But moving forward, we need to be more mindful. Protecting yourself isn't just about what you post, but also about knowing what someone could piece together about you from everything you share."

Reporting and Blocking Suspicious Users

As Aarushi continued, she emphasized that social media platforms often had built-in safety features they could use. "Don't be afraid to report and block people who make you feel uncomfortable or threatened. Reporting sends a message that the behavior isn't acceptable and allows the platform to take action."

Sophia added, "We can't control how everyone behaves online, but we can control how we respond."

Being Aware of Public Wi-Fi Risks

"Another thing to remember is to be cautious when using public Wi-Fi," Aarushi explained. "Public Wi-Fi networks are often less secure, making it easier for hackers to access your data. When you're on a public network, avoid accessing sensitive accounts like banking or email. Use a VPN if possible to encrypt your connection."

Sophia nodded. "I never thought much about public Wi-Fi risks. I'll start using a VPN when I need to connect in public spaces."

Educating Friends and Family

Finally, Aarushi stressed the importance of educating others. "It's great that we're becoming more informed, but it's also essential to pass this knowledge along to our friends and family. The more people who know how to protect themselves, the safer we'll all be."

Kaneera smiled, "Like a ripple effect."

Aarushi returned her smile. "Exactly. Online security isn't just about protecting yourself; it's about creating a culture of awareness."

A Renewed Sense of Security

As they wrapped up their discussion, Aarushi could see a renewed sense of determination on her friends' faces. What had started as a terrifying experience had turned into a lesson in resilience and empowerment. Kaneera and Sophia felt equipped with the knowledge and tools to stand up to their digital adversaries.

Sophia summed it up perfectly. "We may not be able to control everything that happens online, but we can choose how we respond to it. And now, we're ready to face whatever comes our way."

Aarushi nodded in agreement, feeling a quiet satisfaction in knowing they had taken a proactive step toward securing their digital lives.

With their sense of security restored, Aarushi, Kaneera, and Sophia returned to their routines with renewed confidence. But little did they know that the stalker's next move would test everything they had learned. With their guard up and their new strategies in place, they would soon discover the true resilience of their friendship and their determination to remain safe in a world where shadows creep just behind the screen.

Chapter 7: The Dark Web Connection

7.1 Discovery of their Personal Information being sold on the Dark Web

While sitting at the table having lunch and talking about their families and future endeavours, Aarushi stared at her screen in disbelief. What she was seeing shouldn't have been there. Her eyes moved over the screen as a chill ran down her spine. Kaneera was busy scrolling through her phone, and Sophia was busy cooking when Aarushi's voice broke the silence.

"GUYS... YOU NEED TO see this."

Kaneera and Sophia looked up, initially curious but then alarmed by the tension in Aarushi's tone. They moved closer to her laptop, eyes widening as they saw a series of listings on an eerie, unfamiliar website.

"What is this place?" Sophia asked, a hint of dread creeping into her voice.

Aarushi hesitated, then replied, "This... is the dark web. It's a part of the internet most people never see. And it looks like someone is selling our personal information here."

Kaneera gasped. "Our information? Like... my Instagram details or what?"

"More than that," Aarushi answered grimly. "I'm talking about addresses, phone numbers, passwords... things that should be private."

Sophia's face paled as she processed the information. "How can that even be possible? Who would do this?"

Aarushi clenched her jaw, anger mixing with anxiety. "Whoever has been targeting us. This isn't just trolling anymore. Someone is taking our personal details and even selling them here for anyone to buy."

What Is the Dark Web?

Seeing the rising alarm in Kaneera and Sophia's faces, Aarushi took a moment to explain.

"The dark web is a part of the internet that's hidden from search engines and regular browsers. You need special software, like Tor, to access it," she explained. "Not everything on the dark web is illegal, but unfortunately, it's become a place where a lot of shady activities happen-like selling people's information."

Sophia crossed her arms, visibly tense. "So, how did our information even get there? We've been so careful."

Aarushi nodded, feeling the same frustration. "That's the scary part. The person behind this probably has access to more of our personal data than we realized. They may have stolen it from one of our accounts or even tracked our activities without us knowing. There are countless ways personal information can be leaked or stolen, and this person seems to know exactly what they're doing."

The Shock of Exposure

As they scrolled through the listings, they saw the horrifying details on display. Aarushi's address, Kaneera's email associated with her social media accounts, and Sophia's work-related information were meticulously laid out.

"Why would someone want this information?" Kaneera whispered, her voice barely audible.

Aarushi sighed. "People on the dark web buy and sell this data for all sorts of reasons-identity theft, phishing scams, blackmail, even cyberstalking. They're all ways to exploit people and make money."

Sophia's hands clenched into fists. "So we're just... products to them?"

Aarushi nodded solemnly. "To them, yes. Just data they can profit from. This isn't just about privacy anymore; it's about security. They have information that could put us at serious risk."

Uncovering the Cyberstalker's Intent

Aarushi scrolled further, her stomach twisting as she found more connections to their lives. The listings weren't random; they were organized, detailed, and pointed specifically at them. The antagonist's presence was palpable in every line of code, every list of details, as if he were taunting them from behind the screen.

"This isn't just anyone," Aarushi murmured, her face hardening. "Our cyberstalker is someone who knows what they're doing, someone who knows us well enough to gather this much information."

Sophia looked around, her usual calm replaced by an edge of paranoia. "This person has gone from annoying to dangerous. They're no amateur."

Kaneera, still shocked, finally spoke up. "But why would they want to sell our data? Why would they go to these lengths?"

"Money could be part of it, but I think it's more than that," Aarushi replied, her voice low. "It's personal. They're trying to scare us, to keep us on edge. And selling our data is one way to do that. They're showing us that they have control, that they know things we thought were private."

Sophia's eyes narrowed. "So what's our next step?"

Aarushi took a deep breath, her mind racing through possibilities. "First, we need to secure our information. I have a few ideas to help with that. But then... we might need to take things up a level. This isn't just a random attack. This person is going out of their way to hurt us, and they're not going to stop until we take action."

A Plan to Protect Themselves

Determined not to let the cyberstalker continue their control, Aarushi formulated a plan. They would change passwords, enable two-factor authentication on every account, and carefully comb through all their security settings to ensure there were no weak points.

"We need to cover our tracks, check every account, and lock down anything that looks even remotely suspicious," Aarushi said.

They went through their devices, making a list of steps to take. Aarushi emphasized the importance of using unique, complex passwords and not reusing any across accounts. They each enabled two-factor authentication, adding an extra layer of security to every log-in.

"Every step we take matters," Aarushi reminded them. "We're not just trying to protect our accounts; we're trying to reclaim our lives from this person."

The Frustration of the Unseen Enemy

As they worked, Aarushi couldn't shake the sense of being watched. The knowledge that their private lives had been invaded left an unsettling feeling that lingered in the room, casting a shadow over their usual camaraderie.

Sophia voiced what they were all feeling. "It's like there's this invisible line between us and whoever's doing this. They're watching us, but we can't see them."

Aarushi nodded. "That's exactly what they want. They want us to feel vulnerable and helpless. But we're not going to let them win."

Taking Back Control

The three friends worked well into the night, each feeling a renewed sense of purpose. They weren't just reacting to the cyberstalker anymore; they were taking steps to fight back, to regain their sense of security and control.

As they finalized their security measures, Kaneera looked at Aarushi, a hint of defiance in her eyes. "We're not just their victims. We're stronger than that. And we're going to prove it."

Aarushi smiled, her determination mirrored in Sophia's gaze. "Exactly. This is just the beginning. They may have started this, but we're going to end it."

A Message from the Antagonist

Just as they were wrapping up, Aarushi received a message. The words on the screen made her heart skip a beat. It was a message from an anonymous source, a taunting reminder that the cyberstalker was still watching, still waiting.

"You think you're safe? You have no idea what's coming."

The message left them in stunned silence. Aarushi could feel the threat behind every word, the chilling reminder that the cyberstalker was one step ahead.

"We're dealing with someone who won't stop until they get what they want," she whispered. "And I have a feeling this is going to get a lot worse before it gets better."

The trio knows they've crossed into dangerous territory and that the threat isn't going away. As they explore the hidden corners of the internet, they will encounter even more severe risks. In the next section, they'll confront the complexities of cyber scams, recognizing that they're only beginning to uncover the extent of the antagonist's influence.

7.2 Explanation of the Dark Web, How Personal Data is Traded, and How to Protect Yourself

The more Aarushi, Kaneera, and Sophia learned about the dark web, the more unsettling it became. Their initial shock at seeing their information listed for sale transformed into a grim determination to understand this shadowy world and, hopefully, protect themselves from further exposure.

AARUSHI TOOK IT UPON herself to explain the dark web concept to her friends in a way that they could understand, revealing both its terrifying depths and the essential steps to stay safe.

Aarushi began, "You know how you use Google to search for things? Well, Google is only the surface of the internet-just the tip of the iceberg. Beneath it, there's something called the deep web. This is where you'll find databases, private forums, academic resources, and other things you can't access without proper credentials."

Sophia in a guessing gesture. "And then there's the dark web below that?"

Aarushi nodded. "Yes, you are right. The dark web is a part of the deep web that isn't accessible through regular search engines or browsers. You need specific software, like Tor, to even see it. And while the dark web isn't all illegal, it's where a lot of illegal activities happen, like selling personal information, drugs, weapons, and unfortunately... even stolen identities."

Kaneera stunned. "So, people just... go there to buy and sell other people's lives?"

"It's horrifying, but yes," Aarushi replied. "The dark web has its own marketplaces, where personal data is a form of currency. Hackers steal this data from databases, phishing attacks, malware, or weak security practices, and then sell it for profit."

How Data Gets to the Dark Web

"So, how did our information end up here?" Kaneera asked, still visibly shaken.

"Data breaches are one of the main sources," Aarushi explained. "Imagine a company you've given your information to-say, a social media site or a shopping website-gets hacked. If they don't have strong security in place, hackers can access everything: usernames, passwords, emails, phone numbers, and sometimes even financial information."

Sophia weakened. "And people just... buy this information? For what?"

"It's valuable for many reasons," Aarushi continued. "Hackers can use it for identity theft, to open credit lines, to steal money from bank accounts, or even just to stalk someone."

Kaneera gasped. "So... anyone could buy our information and... pretend to be us?"

"Exactly," Aarushi said. "The scarier part is, once data is sold on the dark web, it's hard to control who has it. You might be able to change a password, but you can't always change your email, address, or phone number. And that's why prevention and vigilance are so important."

Common Types of Personal Data Sold on the Dark Web

Aarushi listed out some of the most commonly traded types of data to help them understand the scale of the issue.

Usernames and Passwords: Stolen login credentials are among the most commonly traded items. They're used for account takeovers, where hackers can log in as you and access private information or make unauthorized purchases.

Emails and Contact Information: These are often used for phishing attacks. A hacker with your email can target you with personalized scams that look legitimate.

Social Security Numbers: While less common outside the U.S., this type of data allows someone to assume an identity, open credit accounts, and more.

Financial Information: Credit card numbers, bank account details, and payment methods are especially valuable because they allow direct access to funds.

Medical Records: Surprisingly, medical data is highly valuable. Hackers can use it for insurance fraud or even to blackmail individuals with sensitive health information.

Address and Phone Number: While they might seem harmless, these details can be used for harassment, doxxing, or to make scams appear more authentic.

Kaneera's voice was barely a whisper. "And all this data... it can just be out there for anyone to buy?"

"Yes," Aarushi confirmed. "That's why so many companies are focusing on online security now-to prevent this kind of thing from happening. But even one weak link can expose millions of people."

How Hackers Use This Data

Sophia, always interested in understanding the deeper motives, asked, "So once they have this data, what do they do with it?"

Aarushi explained, "There are different types of hackers with different goals. Some sell data to make money, some use it to commit fraud, and others might use it for harassment or blackmail. For example, if someone has enough of your information, they can impersonate you to access your accounts or take over your identity for their own gain."

Kaneera looked alarmed. "So this isn't just about privacy-it's about safety, right?"

"Absolutely," Aarushi said. "Hackers might use the data to harass someone directly, or they could even sell it to a stalker or someone with bad intentions. That's why protecting our data is so crucial."

How to Protect Yourself from Dark Web Data Leaks

"So, what do we do?" Sophia asked, determined to take action.

"First, let's talk about some basic practices," Aarushi replied, pulling up a list on her laptop.

1. Use Strong, Unique Passwords

Aarushi emphasized that using the same password across different accounts made it easy for hackers to gain access to multiple platforms. "If you're using the same password for social media, email, and banking, one data breach could expose everything," she warned. "Always create unique passwords and, if possible, use a password manager to keep track of them."

2. Enable Two-Factor Authentication (2FA)

"Adding two-factor authentication is like adding another layer of security," Aarushi explained. "Even if someone has your password, they'd need a second form of verification, like a code sent to your phone, to get in."

3. Be Cautious with Personal Information Online

"It's tempting to share everything on social media, but the more information you share, the easier it is for hackers to piece together your identity," she continued. "Be mindful of sharing your location, daily routines, or personal details that could give hackers clues about your life."

4. Regularly Monitor Your Accounts

"Check your financial statements and online accounts regularly," Aarushi advised. "Look for any strange activity, and report it immediately if you see anything suspicious."

5. Use Encrypted Communication

Sophia was intrigued by this. Aarushi explained, "There are messaging apps that use end-to-end encryption, which means that only the sender and receiver can read the messages. This can help protect you if someone tries to intercept your communications."

6. Run Regular Security Checks on Your Devices

"A lot of hackers gain access through malware or spyware, so it's essential to run regular scans on your devices," Aarushi said. "This can help catch anything suspicious before it becomes a bigger issue."

Additional Steps to Safeguard Personal Data

After covering the basics, Aarushi delved into a few advanced methods for securing data.

1. Check for Data Breaches

Aarushi suggested they check whether their emails or passwords had been compromised in past data breaches. "There are websites that can tell you if your email has been part of a breach," she said. "It's a good way to know if you need to change any passwords."

2. Avoid Using Public Wi-Fi for Sensitive Transactions

"Hackers can intercept information sent over public Wi-Fi," she explained. "When you're connected to public networks, avoid logging into important accounts or making transactions."

3. Use a VPN

"A virtual private network (VPN) encrypts your internet traffic and hides your IP address," Aarushi continued. "This can help keep your activity private, especially if you're using public networks or accessing sites that may track your data."

4. Freeze Your Credit

Sophia was surprised to hear about this option. "If you're really concerned about identity theft, you can freeze your credit," Aarushi told them. "It makes it harder for someone to open new accounts in your name."

Understanding the Consequences of Data Theft

Sophia looked thoughtful. "So... if people don't take these precautions, they're putting themselves at risk?"

Aarushi nodded. "Unfortunately, yes. And it's not just about money or privacy. If someone gains enough of your personal information, they could potentially ruin your life. They could impersonate you, steal your identity, and even cause trouble with the law."

Kaneera looked horrified. "And once it's on the dark web, it's there forever, right?"

"Pretty much," Aarushi confirmed. "Data is rarely deleted. Once it's out there, it can be passed around, sold, and resold. That's why prevention is so critical."

Staying Attentive and Empowered

Aarushi's words made a deep impression on her friends. They realized that, while they couldn't fully control what happened to their data, they could take measures to protect themselves and stay cautious.

"Our information is valuable, and we need to treat it that way," Aarushi said, her tone firm. "From now on, we're going to be proactive, not just reactive. We can't change the past, but we can protect our future."

With a renewed sense of determination, the trio agreed to follow the steps Aarushi had outlined. They knew they couldn't erase their data from the dark web, but they could at least fortify their defenses and stay ahead of future threats.

As Aarushi, Kaneera, and Sophia take these measures, they understand that this will not stop anytime soon. Their journey through the dark web's impact on their lives has given them a clearer picture of the power and dangers of the digital world.

7.3 Aarushi Starts Tracking Down the Cybercriminal Responsible

With each unsettling revelation, Aarushi's determination grew. Their information being listed on the dark web was one thing, but knowing it was being sold and distributed meant they were caught in someone's deliberate scheme. And that realization stirred something in Aarushi: the instinct to fight back. She wasn't just going to sit by and let someone terrorize her and her friends. She was going to track down the cybercriminal responsible.

SETTING UP THE HUNT

Aarushi settled in front of her laptop, a newfound sense of purpose and focus sharpening her gaze. The light from her screen illuminated her face as she opened her investigative tools, software she had once used for academic projects now becoming weapons in her mission.

Kaneera and Sophia sat nearby, watching with a mix of amazement and worry. They trusted Aarushi, but this was an entirely new level of online security, one that felt dangerous yet empowering.

"Are you sure this is safe?" Sophia asked cautiously.

Aarushi gave her a reassuring nod. "Yes, I'll be careful. We're not doing anything illegal. I'm just gathering information-looking for patterns, tracing breadcrumbs. Whoever is behind this didn't just choose us by chance. They left clues, and I'm going to find them."

She started by analyzing the profiles that had been leaving odd comments and following Kaneera's accounts. "Sometimes, even the smallest detail can reveal more than you'd think," Aarushi explained. "It could be an IP address, a username used across different platforms, or even a distinctive pattern in their writing."

She began cross-referencing usernames, dates, and locations. Every click and keystroke felt like uncovering a hidden clue in a complex puzzle. Aarushi's mind whirred, recalling the digital forensics skills she'd studied. Each bit of information had the potential to connect her to the cybercriminal responsible.

Identifying Patterns in the Cybercriminal's Behavior

Aarushi noticed something peculiar in the data she'd gathered so far. The comments left on Kaneera's profiles, the emails, and even some of the threats Sophia had received-they all seemed to appear at the same time of day. It was as though the person responsible operated on a strict schedule, leaving their malicious digital footprint between certain hours.

"This timing pattern... it's almost like this person has a routine," Aarushi muttered, more to herself than her friends.

Sophia leaned in, intrigued. "A routine? So, like... a job?"

"Exactly," Aarushi replied. "Or maybe they're accessing the internet only at certain times, which could mean they're working around something else, like a day job or a specific time zone. This helps narrow things down."

Aarushi's tech skills enabled her to uncover some preliminary information: the cybercriminal seemed to be using a VPN to mask their location, changing it frequently to avoid detection. However, there was one location that popped up repeatedly-a possible slip-up on the criminal's part.

"Do you see this?" Aarushi pointed to a recurring IP address that showed up from time to time. "It's masked, but I can tell this person slips up and sometimes forgets to cover their tracks fully. They're human, after all."

Kaneera and Sophia watched in astonishment as Aarushi pieced together the cybercriminal's behavioral patterns, slowly revealing the digital trail leading them to the next step.

Tracing the Dark Web Connections

The deeper Aarushi went, the more she understood how the dark web operated. Transactions, she realized, were happening with relative anonymity, thanks to cryptocurrency. This anonymity made it nearly impossible to identify the person purchasing or selling their data.

Aarushi explained this to her friends, noting how the dark web's reliance on cryptocurrency for anonymity made it both powerful and dangerous. "But even though they're using cryptocurrency, there are still ways to trace transactions, at least partially," she said. "There's a chance I can find the wallets connected to our data."

Using blockchain analysis tools, Aarushi began investigating transactions associated with the digital wallet that seemed to be involved in selling their data. Each time she encountered a new wallet address, she cross-referenced it with public blockchain data, slowly untangling a web of transactions and hidden identities. It was tedious and complex work, but Aarushi's focus was unwavering.

"This wallet has been active recently," Aarushi observed, "which means our data is still fresh to them. Whoever this is, they're not done with us."

Diving Deeper: The Person behind the Screen

Through a combination of blockchain analysis and some calculated digital plots, Aarushi finally uncovered something critical. One of the cryptocurrency wallets, connected to their data, had also been used to make purchases from a seemingly unrelated site-one where usernames and partial email addresses were occasionally visible.

With a triumphant grin, Aarushi pulled up a profile. "Here it is," she announced. "This username matches one of the profiles leaving strange comments on Kaneera's posts."

They now had a pseudonym-a small but significant clue that might help them uncover more.

The pseudonym seemed familiar, but Aarushi couldn't place it at first. Then it struck her-she'd seen a similar name connected to several online security forums and dark web chatrooms. She dove deeper, scrolling through old forum posts, piecing together fragments of conversations and finding connections to various hacker communities.

After what felt like hours, Aarushi finally found a lead. The cybercriminal had left an unmistakable signature, something unique in their writing style and the way they talked about certain attacks.

A Digital Confrontation

Armed with this information, Aarushi considered the next move carefully. She knew that reaching out to this person directly would be dangerous, yet she felt compelled to confront them. But instead of directly messaging the individual, she crafted a warning and placed it strategically on one of the forums where she'd seen them active.

"You thought you could scare us, but you underestimated what we're capable of. We know more about you than you think. We're watching you now."

Kaneera and Sophia gasped as they watched her type the message. "Are you sure that's a good idea?" Kaneera asked nervously.

Aarushi hesitated for a moment, feeling the weight of her decision. "It's a risk, but I want them to know we're not as helpless as they think."

Within minutes, there was a response.

"Bold move. But you don't know what you're getting into. Walk away while you still can."

The message sent a chill down Aarushi's spine, but she remained composed. The response revealed a hint of arrogance, a trait she could exploit.

Protecting Themselves While Moving Forward

After the exchange, Aarushi knew that the situation had escalated. This wasn't just about defending against passive threats anymore-this was a confrontation with someone who was skilled, cunning, and possibly vengeful.

To protect themselves, she set up extra layers of security. They used encrypted messaging for all their conversations, updated their passwords, enabled two-factor authentication on every possible account, and kept backup copies of critical data offline.

She also installed tracking software on her laptop, allowing her to monitor any unusual activity and spot further attempts from the cybercriminal.

"This is more than just a game to them," Aarushi said solemnly. "They're trying to send a message. But so are we-we're saying we won't back down."

A Glimpse of the Antagonist

As they continued to strengthen their defenses, Aarushi stumbled upon another eerie detail. One of the usernames she had identified led her to a public post-a post that detailed specific attacks and "projects" this person had worked on. The language was clinical, almost detached, yet there was an underlying thrill to the words as if the person revelled in their digital exploits.

"This person... they're not just an ordinary hacker," Aarushi whispered. "They're someone who enjoys watching others squirm."

It was becoming clear that these individuals weren't just after their data; they enjoyed the power they wielded over their targets. Kaneera and Sophia exchanged worried glances, realizing the gravity of their situation.

Sophia, ever the pragmatist, asked, "So, what do we do now? Do we keep trying to track them down, or...?"

Aarushi's gaze was steely as she replied, "We continue. We're not alone in this anymore, but we're not stopping either. If anything, this is only pushing me to learn more about them. They might think they're in control, but we're going to show them otherwise."

With this renewed determination, the trio realized they were dealing with a truly dangerous adversary, one who had now crossed the line from digital threats to psychological warfare. In the following chapter, they will explore more deeply their newfound mission, ready to confront the next wave of challenges, from advanced social engineering tactics to the secrets lurking within hidden data exchanges. Their battle wasn't over-it was only beginning.

Chapter 8: The Hacker's Trap

8.1 Aarushi Devises a Plan to Lure the Hacker Out

As their unseen adversary's presence grew bolder, Aarushi's resolve hardened. She'd been quietly studying the hacker's methods and patterns, learning how he stalked through digital spaces, always one step ahead. But Aarushi was done letting this person hold the power. If they were going to get any answers-and possibly even some peace-she knew she'd have to take a risk. She was ready to lure him out.

Mapping out the Hacker's Digital Behavior

Over the past few days, Aarushi had meticulously tracked the hacker's activities, noting specific times and methods he favored. It seemed he operated with an almost ritualistic precision, often using similar entry points to peek into their accounts or send intimidating messages.

She realized that the hacker enjoyed taunting them, waiting for a response to fuel his control over them. He left clues here and there, daring them to engage. This arrogance was something Aarushi could use to her advantage.

"We need to think a step ahead," she explained to Kaneera and Sophia as they gathered in her apartment. The soft glow from her computer illuminated the room, casting a determined look on Aarushi's face.

Kaneera is concerned. "How do we plan to trap someone who's already so good at covering his tracks?"

Aarushi gave her a slight, reassuring smile. "Everyone has a weak point, even the most cautious hacker. And I think I've found his."

She opened her laptop, showing her friends a string of dates and times when the hacker had last interacted with their accounts. "He's not as invisible as he thinks," Aarushi said confidently. "There's a pattern here. He logs in regularly-around 1:00 a.m. our time-and uses similar proxy locations. He's trying to stay anonymous, but he's making the same moves repeatedly."

Kaneera and Sophia watched with a mix of amazement and apprehension. "So you think we can use this against him?"

Aarushi nodded. "Yes. We'll set a digital trap that looks too tempting for him to resist."

Setting up the Trap

With her plan forming, Aarushi got to work, detailing every step carefully. She knew that it would require a bait account-a seemingly vulnerable entry point that the hacker would feel compelled to exploit. She decided to create a fake profile that mimicked Kaneera's, one with just enough enticing details to draw him in.

"This account will look almost like yours, Kaneera," Aarushi explained. "It'll have a few posts, some casual selfies, and one big vulnerability: a 'mistake' that leaves her contact info visible."

Kaneera surprised but agreed. "You mean something that would make him think I've slipped up again?"

"Exactly," Aarushi confirmed. "This bait account will look like an easy target-too easy for him to resist. I'll give it some posts that seem careless and add a few hints of insecurity in the captions, things that would signal he can get into it easily."

Sophia nodded in understanding. "We're making him feel like he's the one in control. He won't suspect he's the one being watched."

Layered Defenses

Aarushi didn't stop with just a fake account; she carefully installed multiple tracking software on the fake account to alert her as soon as any suspicious activity occurred. By embedding hidden tags and subtle markers, she could trace the hacker's movements as he steered through the account, revealing his preferred techniques and any proxy networks he used.

Aarushi explained, "I'm setting it up so that every click he makes, every message he reads, will silently alert me to his location, his IP address-even details about his browser."

Sophia looked impressed. "That's genius, Aarushi. So it's like we're creating a trap that works in layers?"

"Exactly. This is designed to give us as much intel as possible," Aarushi replied. "With each layer, we'll get closer to understanding who he is and, ideally, where he's operating from."

The Anticipation of the Trap

Once the bait account was ready, they all felt a shift in the air. It was the first time they weren't just reacting to the hacker-they were actively drawing him in. Aarushi stayed up late, watching her screen with quiet intensity, her heart racing every time a new notification popped up.

Finally, at exactly 1:00 a.m., Aarushi's laptop pinged. The hacker had taken the bait.

"He's here," she whispered to her friends, who had dozed off on her couch but woke instantly at her voice.

As Aarushi tracked the hacker's movements, she noted how he navigated through the fake account, almost instinctively knowing where to look. He went straight for the personal information section, scrolling and examining each detail Aarushi had meticulously curated to seem carelessly exposed.

But her eyes narrowed as she noticed something odd-the hacker was taking screenshots.

"Aarushi, what's he doing?" Kaneera asked, worry clouding her face.

"He's making copies of the 'sensitive' information I left. He's taking the bait fully. This is exactly what we needed," Aarushi replied, her hands steady on the keyboard. The hacker's every click and keystroke left a trail she could follow.

A Suspicious Email from the Hacker

Then, as Aarushi tracked his activity, her inbox pinged with a new message. It was from an unknown email address-one that looked suspiciously similar to other addresses the hacker had used to send threatening messages before.

The email subject read, "I know your secrets."

Kaneera leaned over, reading the email with wide eyes. "Does he actually think he's hacked into your real account?"

"Let's hope so," Aarushi replied with a smirk. "He's acting exactly as I'd hoped."

The email contained a message laced with intimidation: "You thought you could hide from me? I know more than you think. Every detail you're trying to keep private... I'll expose it. Unless, of course, you're willing to cooperate."

Kaneera looked at Aarushi, a mixture of fear and excitement on her face. "This is our chance, Aarushi. We have to push him further."

Aarushi nodded. "It's time to respond. But on our terms."

The Digital Chess Match

Crafting her reply carefully, Aarushi kept her tone vague yet confident, hinting that she was "interested in a truce." She sent back a short message that simply said, "You seem to know a lot. Let's talk. I want to understand what you're looking for."

She watched as the hacker typed a reply almost immediately, his eagerness betraying him. They continued exchanging messages, with Aarushi gradually leading him into questions that would reveal more about his motives and background.

Sophia, who had been quietly observing, finally spoke. "This is brilliant, Aarushi. You're getting him to reveal more than he realizes."

It didn't take long before the hacker slipped up, revealing that he was working with certain tools that Aarushi recognized. Each detail, no matter how small, helped her map out his techniques, his strategies, and, most importantly, his vulnerabilities.

Securing Proof of the Hacker's Identity

Through their exchanges, Aarushi was able to embed a small tracer within her messages-software that would help track his exact location should he open the message on his personal device. They knew this might be the only chance to pinpoint his whereabouts, so Aarushi carefully crafted a message filled with just enough bait to ensure he would open it without hesitation.

After sending the message, Aarushi watched her tracking software, her heart racing as she waited for it to activate. Within moments, the signal pinged. Her screen showed a location-a physical address. The hacker was accessing his account from a neighborhood across town.

Aarushi's mind whirled with this revelation. "He's closer than we thought," she said, her voice barely a whisper.

The Trap is Unleashed

With the address in hand, Aarushi contacted local authorities, carefully explaining the situation and providing all the digital proof they'd gathered. Though questioning at first, the authorities couldn't deny the substantial evidence Aarushi presented. They agreed to look into it and thanked her for her meticulous work.

As she closed her laptop that night, Aarushi looked at Kaneera and Sophia with a sense of victory. "We did it. We've got him on our radar now."

The girls shared a relieved smile, knowing they had taken a significant step toward reclaiming control. But Aarushi also knew that this victory came with a warning-whoever their hacker was, he was close and likely wouldn't take being exposed lightly.

With the hacker's identity on the verge of being revealed, Aarushi, Kaneera, and Sophia brace themselves for what's next. In the following sections, they'll dive even deeper into uncovering his motives, tracking his connections, and facing the possibility that he might retaliate. Their journey into the world of online security is no longer just about protecting themselves; it's about ensuring that no one else falls victim to the same trap.

8.2 Explanation of Ethical Hacking, Tracing IPs, and Monitoring Digital Footprints

Aarushi leaned forward, her fingers tapping on the laptop's keyboard as she prepared to explain her next move to Kaneera and Sophia. After laying the bait for the hacker, she knew it was time to go over some foundational concepts with her friends-especially given how unnerving their situation had become. The hacker had become a shadow in their lives, and it was only through ethical hacking techniques that Aarushi could hope to expose him without stepping outside the law.

"ETHICAL HACKING IS essentially using hacking skills for good," Aarushi began, sensing her friend's curiosity. "It's about understanding the mindset of a hacker to prevent malicious attacks and to protect people like us."

Sophia nodded thoughtfully. "So it's like getting into the mind of a criminal to catch one?"

"Exactly," Aarushi agreed. "And it's not just about gathering information-it's about doing it legally and ethically, which is crucial. There's a line between using your skills to help others and crossing into a territory that could be harmful."

Ethical Hacking: A Brief Overview

Aarushi explained that ethical hackers, sometimes called "white-hat" hackers, are skilled professionals who use hacking techniques to protect individuals, businesses, and governments from online threats. They work with the permission of their targets, often testing the security of a system to identify weaknesses before real attackers can exploit them.

"Think of it as a preventative measure," Aarushi explained. "By hacking into a system with the owner's consent, ethical hackers can find vulnerabilities and fix them. It's like a doctor diagnosing a patient to prevent an illness from getting worse."

Kaneera looked intrigued. "So, ethical hackers basically use the same skills as regular hackers?"

"Yes, but with a major difference in intent and boundaries," Aarushi replied. "While unethical hackers-those we call 'black-hats'-use these skills for financial gain, revenge, or power, ethical hackers follow strict rules. They operate within legal guidelines and respect people's privacy."

Sophia seemed impressed. "So by setting up that bait account, you were essentially acting like an ethical hacker?"

"Exactly," Aarushi replied. "I'm staying within the law but using tactics that can help us defend ourselves and identify our attacker."

Tracing IPs: Finding the Hacker's Digital Location

To further educate her friends, Aarushi dove into one of the primary tools for identifying cyber intruders: IP tracing. Every device connected to the internet has an IP address-a unique series of numbers that indicate where it's connected from. She pulled up a visualization of an IP address, showing how it could be traced back to general regions, service providers, and sometimes even closer locations.

"IP addresses are like digital footprints," she explained. "When you connect to a website or send a message, your IP address leaves a mark. It's like leaving a signature every time you go online."

Kaneera looked down. "But can't hackers hide their IPs?"

"They often try," Aarushi acknowledged. "Hackers use proxies, VPNs, or even multiple layers of servers to disguise their true location. But even the best hackers sometimes slip up. They might connect to the wrong network, forget to mask an IP, or leave traces that, with patience, we can follow."

She continued, "The hacker who's been after us has been fairly careful, but the bait account gave us the chance to catch him slipping. By tracing the IP connected to our fake account, I was able to see hints of where he might be located."

Sophia leaned in. "So you're saying every time he interacted with the bait, he risked exposing himself?"

"Yes. Each time he accessed that account, it gave me more data points, more IPs to work with," Aarushi explained. "It's like slowly piecing together a trail he didn't realize he was leaving."

Digital Footprints: Understanding Online Traces

After explaining IPs, Aarushi shifted to the concept of digital footprints. Every action taken online leaves a trail that, when pieced together, can tell a story. This includes things like browsing history, social media interactions, email metadata, and more.

"A digital footprint is the collective record of your online behavior," Aarushi elaborated. "Most of us don't think about it, but every click, like, or comment can be tracked. The more we engage online, the bigger the footprint we leave behind."

Kaneera looked concerned. "So does that mean someone could track us the same way we're tracking this hacker?"

"Yes, but with some differences," Aarushi replied. "Digital footprints can be harder to erase than we think, but they're not all easily accessible. With strong privacy settings and careful behavior, we can control much of the footprint we leave."

She added, "It's also why ethical hackers and online security experts stress the importance of privacy settings, avoiding public Wi-Fi, and limiting the amount of personal information shared online."

The Ethical Boundaries of Tracking

As they discussed more, Aarushi stressed the ethical boundaries that distinguish responsible tracking from invasion of privacy. "There's a line between gathering information to protect ourselves and crossing into territory where we could be invading someone else's privacy. As much as we want to stop this hacker, we have to be careful not to overstep."

Sophia nodded. "It's like you're staying within the law even while trying to stop someone who isn't."

"Correct," Aarushi replied. "That's the difference between ethical hacking and hacking for harm. It's about accountability."

Tools and Techniques for Tracing

Aarushi described some common tools and techniques used for IP tracking and monitoring digital footprints, all while emphasizing that these methods were only to be used legally and ethically.

- **IP Lookup Tools:** Aarushi explained that there were tools available that allowed users to perform a lookup on any IP address to determine its general location. She showed an example of a map that displayed the rough area an IP was coming from.
- **WHOIS Lookups:** This is a tool that allows users to learn more about the ownership and origin of an IP address. Although not perfect, it could reveal the name of the internet service provider or the company that owned a specific IP range.
- **Digital Fingerprinting:** Aarushi explained that digital fingerprinting was an advanced technique used to create a unique profile based on a user's device, browser, and browsing habits. This can help identify a user even if they switch devices or IP addresses.
- **Cookies and Metadata:** Aarushi highlighted that cookies and metadata could provide information on a user's browsing habits, helping to create a fuller picture of their online activity. While primarily used in marketing, metadata can sometimes be used to detect suspicious patterns.

Tracking the Hacker Ethically

Armed with these tools, Aarushi worked carefully to monitor the hacker's behavior without crossing any ethical boundaries. She limited her actions to her own bait account, gathering only information that the hacker had knowingly accessed.

Each IP address that the hacker used added a new point to her map, slowly creating a pattern she could analyze. She could see that he tended to connect from specific locations and that he often checked the bait account at similar times.

"This pattern shows us more about his routine," Aarushi told her friends. "Even though he thinks he's in control, we're watching him."

Precautions While Tracking

As she worked, Aarushi emphasized to her friends the importance of caution. "When you're tracking someone, it's vital to ensure your own digital safety. I'm using secure networks, multiple firewalls, and constantly monitoring my own IP to ensure he doesn't detect our efforts."

Kaneera looked anxious. “So he might still be watching us while we’re watching him?”

“It’s possible,” Aarushi admitted, “but I’ve set up our accounts and devices to be as secure as possible. This is why being careful with your digital footprint is so crucial.”

Turning the Tables: Monitoring His Next Steps

With the hacker’s pattern becoming clearer, Aarushi explained her next plan. “Once we have enough data points, we’ll be able to predict his moves better. Ethical hacking isn’t just about reacting; it’s about anticipating the attacker’s next steps.”

By carefully monitoring the hacker’s digital footprint, Aarushi would have the opportunity to potentially block him from accessing sensitive accounts or even report his IP addresses to authorities as a preventive measure.

Sophia looked impressed. “So this isn’t just about defense-it’s about going on the offense without crossing any lines.”

“Right,” Aarushi confirmed. “The goal of ethical hacking is to prevent harm by staying one step ahead.”

The Risks of Tracing a Hacker

Aarushi reminded her friends that while tracking their hacker, they were operating in a world where risks existed. Hackers were often aware of digital traps and could retaliate if they felt cornered.

“That’s why we’re being extremely cautious,” she said, her tone serious. “This isn’t a game. This person could lash out if they suspect we’re on to them. Our goal is to gather enough information to report him without provoking him.”

With each new IP tracked and every digital footprint examined, Aarushi was getting closer to piecing together the hacker’s identity. In the next section, her pursuit would deepen as she explored the hacker’s connections, discovering a network of individuals tied to the dark web. With the stakes rising, Aarushi, Kaneera, and Sophia would have to confront not only their attacker but also the hidden layers of an underground cybercriminal network.

8.3 The Confrontation: Aarushi and Sophia Face off against the Cybercriminal

The night was quiet, the faint hum of the city beneath the open window the only background noise in Aarushi's small apartment. Sitting side-by-side with Sophia, Aarushi's eyes remained fixed on her screen as she watched the virtual trail they'd spent days constructing lead them to their attacker's lair-digitally speaking. Weeks of gathering data, piecing together fragments of the hacker's identity, and laying traps in the digital landscape had all come to this moment.

"Aarushi, are you sure about this?" Sophia asked, her voice a blend of caution and resolve. The reality of what they were doing weighed heavily on her. They were about to confront a person who had invaded their lives, someone who had crossed every line and violated their privacy in ways unimaginable. This wasn't just a online chase anymore-it was personal.

Aarushi nodded, her fingers hovering over the keyboard. "I've prepared for this. We've mapped his online activity, we've recorded every digital breadcrumb he left behind, and we know exactly where he'll log in next. This is our chance to stop him before he can hurt anyone else."

Sophia took a steadying breath, steeling herself. "Then let's do this."

SETTING THE TRAP: THE Final Steps

The plan was straightforward but risky. Aarushi had set up a decoy account, mimicking her own profile and baiting the hacker with information he couldn't resist. The account was laced with subtle signals meant to draw him in-posts about her whereabouts, unprotected documents, and details she knew would attract him. What he didn't know was that every move he made would be tracked.

As they waited, Aarushi explained her strategy to Sophia. "He'll be expecting the same lack of security he's seen on my other accounts, but this one is different. The moment he tries to access it, he'll trigger a signal I've set up to track his IP address and digital footprint in real time."

Sophia nodded. "We'll know exactly where he is and who he is."

Aarushi's setup wasn't just about tracking. She'd coded a backdoor to her own decoy account, a virtual trap that would immediately isolate the hacker's connection. If everything went according to plan, they would have enough evidence to bring him to justice.

As expected, the hacker took the bait. A notification blinked on Aarushi's screen, indicating that the decoy account had been accessed. Aarushi's fingers flew across the keyboard as she initiated the backdoor sequence, her eyes darting between the screen and the notification. She could feel Sophia's nervous energy beside her, both of them leaning forward, tense with anticipation.

"He's in," Aarushi whispered, a fierce sense of satisfaction in her voice. "Now we watch."

Unmasking the Attacker

Within moments, Aarushi's program began gathering information. IP addresses, connection points, browsing history-all of it streamed onto her screen in rapid succession. The hacker was skilled, and he attempted to scramble his signals and cover his tracks. But Aarushi's setup was too advanced; she'd anticipated his every move.

With each passing second, more details about their cyberstalker came into focus. Sophia watched in awe as Aarushi traced the hacker's steps, piecing together a digital footprint that unravelled his identity.

Suddenly, a name appeared on the screen-a pseudonym connected to various online forums, dark web marketplaces, and chat rooms known for illegal activity. But Aarushi's software went further, revealing a connection to a real-world IP address.

"There he is," Aarushi breathed. "We've got him."

Sophia's eyes widened. "Are you serious? After all this time, we finally know who he is?"

Aarushi nodded, her face set in a determined expression. "And now we confront him."

Confronting the Cybercriminal

With the hacker's location pinpointed, Aarushi initiated a secure connection to his active chat handle. She typed a message, sending it straight to his screen: "I know who you are. We're watching."

There was a pause on the other end as the hacker took in her message. The seconds ticked by, the tension in the room thick enough to cut.

Sophia held her breath, her eyes glued to the screen, wondering how he would respond.

Then, a reply appeared: "You don't scare me. I know more about you than you think."

Aarushi's face hardened. She typed back, maintaining her composure: "Maybe, but I've got something you don't-proof. And I'm not afraid to use it."

The hacker's response was quick and mocking: "You think you're the first to try this? You're in way over your head."

Sophia whispered, "What now?"

Aarushi's gaze was steely. "Now, we play his game."

She continued to message him, dropping hints that she'd gathered more evidence than she actually had, coaxing him to reveal more about his methods. Bit by bit, his responses grew more defensive, the bravado slipping as he realized he'd underestimated her.

The Hacker's Slip

In his attempt to counter her, the hacker made a critical error. He referenced an account and a set of details only someone with physical access to their devices would know. Aarushi seized on this mistake.

She typed swiftly: "So you admit you accessed our personal files?"

A long pause followed, and then he responded, "What does it matter? I've already taken what I need."

Aarushi smirked, glancing at Sophia. "That's all the confirmation we needed."

Sophia's voice trembled with a mix of anger and relief. "That's it. He just confessed."

Aarushi saved every message, taking screenshots and recording the entire conversation as evidence. She had him, not just with digital proof but a confession that would hold up under investigation.

Revealing the Consequences

Finally, Aarushi decided it was time to let him know the full extent of his predicament. She typed: "We have your IP, your location, your activity logs. The authorities have everything they need."

The hacker's confidence wavered, his responses growing erratic. He tried to backpedal, insisting that he hadn't meant any harm that he was just "playing around." But Aarushi was unyielding. She knew the damage he'd caused-the invasion of privacy, the emotional toll, the constant fear and uncertainty. She wasn't about to let him walk away unaffected.

Sophia added her own message to the chat: "Whatever game you thought you were playing, it's over. You're not getting away with this."

With one final message, Aarushi delivered her parting shot: "Consider this your last warning. Next time, it won't just be us."

The screen went silent, and the hacker's connection abruptly cut. They watched as his online presence vanished, a virtual escape that signalled his defeat. But it didn't matter. They had everything they needed.

Aftermath: The Closure They Needed

As the reality of their victory settled in, Aarushi and Sophia exchanged relieved smiles. They'd done it. They'd faced the faceless figure who had tormented them, and they had won.

Sophia exhaled, finally releasing the tension that had been building up for weeks. "I can't believe it's over."

Aarushi leaned back, a sense of calm washing over her. "It's over because we didn't back down. We stood our ground."

They filed a report with all the evidence they'd gathered, ensuring that law enforcement would be alerted to the hacker's identity and activity. As they sent off the final documentation, Aarushi felt a weight lift from her shoulders. They'd turned the tables on their stalker, and in doing so, they'd taken back control over their lives.

The Lessons Learned

With the hacker exposed, Aarushi, Sophia, and Kaneera met to discuss everything they'd gone through. They had faced an ordeal that had tested their resilience, their friendship, and their understanding of digital safety. In the end, they emerged stronger, more aware, and more prepared to protect themselves from future threats.

Aarushi looked at her friends, her voice resolute. "This won't be the last time we face challenges online, but we know how to protect ourselves now. And we'll be ready."

Sophia smiled. "And if anyone dares to mess with us again, they'll know exactly who they're dealing with."

Their ordeal had forged them into something more resilient, a team bound by trust, determination, and the lessons they'd learned in the face of a relentless digital enemy.

As the dust settled on their confrontation with the cybercriminal, the three friends emerged with a newfound strength and understanding. But while their immediate threat had been neutralized, the digital world continued to evolve, posing new challenges and uncovering new mysteries to be solved. In the next chapter, Aarushi and her friends will explore the deeper implications of digital security and privacy, arming themselves with knowledge and strategies to stay safe in a world where the lines between online and offline continue to blur.

Chapter 9: Taking Back Control

9.1 Aarushi and Sophia Expose the Hacker and Take Back Control

The tension in Aarushi's room was almost evident as she, Kaneera, and Sophia sat around her laptop, eyes fixed on the screen. They were close-closer than they had ever been-to exposing the cybercriminal who had been relentlessly targeting them. With a mix of excitement and dread, Aarushi prepared herself for the final phase of the plan.

Over the last few weeks, she and Sophia had been quietly gathering evidence, each step revealing more about their antagonist's methods and motives. It hadn't been easy, but every setback had only made them more determined. The hacker had gone too far this time, and they were ready to confront him and, ultimately, reclaim their digital lives.

THE CLOCK STRUCK MIDNIGHT, and Aarushi's screen glowed with activity. She typed commands quickly, setting up a virtual environment and preparing a last layer of protection before launching the next stage of her plan. This time, they were taking the offensive.

"Everything ready on your end, Sophia?" Aarushi asked, her tone both calm and determined.

Sophia nodded, glancing down at her notebook filled with carefully documented details of the hacker's trail, along with legal insights she had gathered to reinforce their case. "Ready. Let's do this."

Setting the Trap

In the previous chapter, Aarushi had gathered enough information to locate the hacker's digital footprint. She was able to track his IP address to a hidden server, his virtual base for launching attacks and hosting personal information he had stolen from others. It was a fortress in the digital realm, but Aarushi had discovered one weakness-a backdoor that the hacker, in his arrogance, had overlooked.

She quickly set up a phishing lure specifically crafted to exploit that weakness. The plan was simple but effective: lure him into accessing a decoy file, embedded with code that would trace his location. Aarushi sent it from a burner account, one she created just for this moment, and leaned back, waiting. Her heart pounded as they watched, knowing this might be their one shot to expose him fully.

After a few tense minutes, Aarushi's screen lit up with a notification. The hacker had taken the bait. She quickly started tracking his movements in real-time, a string of code on her screen translating into valuable data. The hacker was online, fully active, and falling into her trap.

"Got him," Aarushi whispered, feeling both exhilaration and relief. "We have his network details-everything we need to identify him."

Confronting the Hacker

Sophia, eyes widening, nodded in encouragement. "Let's make sure he realizes he messed with the wrong people."

Aarushi quickly pulled up the hacker's login credentials and worked on locking him out of the servers he had been using to store their data. As she deleted the files he had collected on them, she left a single message on his server:

"You tried to play a game you couldn't win. Consider this game over."

A few seconds later, Aarushi received an incoming message from the hacker. It was short, filled with bravado and insults, a last-ditch attempt to intimidate them. But Aarushi, persistent, simply sent back a screenshot of his own network details-the ultimate power move. It was a direct message that the tables had turned, and they were in control now.

For the first time in weeks, Aarushi felt a surge of confidence, a sense of relief. The hacker's response was silence. They had finally managed to take back what he had stolen from them: their security, their control, and their peace of mind.

Restoring Their Privacy and Security

With the hacker neutralized and his files wiped clean, Aarushi and Sophia focused on restoring their accounts and reinforcing their privacy settings. Aarushi guided Kaneera through the steps of securing her social media profiles, enabling advanced privacy settings, and implementing two-factor authentication on all her accounts.

"We need to make sure nothing like this happens again," Aarushi said, looking at both Kaneera and Sophia with determination. She explained the importance of layered security and how to review account permissions, emphasizing that taking proactive steps was the only way to stay truly protected.

Sophia, ever practical, had already outlined a report to send to local authorities detailing the events and the hacker's information. She knew the legal system wasn't flawless, but at least they could ensure the hacker would face the consequences.

Kaneera, who had been quiet throughout most of the process, finally spoke up. "I never thought about how vulnerable I was. Thank you, both of you," she said, her voice filled with genuine gratitude.

"You're one of us, Kaneera," Aarushi said with a reassuring smile. "We'll always have each other's backs."

Moving Forward

With their accounts locked down and the hacker's trail documented, the three friends took a moment to reflect on everything they had been through. The experience had changed them-not just in terms of their understanding of online security but in how they saw the world. They were no longer passive users of technology; they were now active, cautious, and informed.

"You know," Sophia said, leaning back thoughtfully, "this whole thing makes me want to do more. Maybe we can start something-an online awareness campaign or something to teach others about digital security."

Aarushi nodded, her eyes lighting up with enthusiasm. "That's a great idea, Sophia. If we can help even one person avoid what we went through, it'll be worth it."

Kaneera laughed. "Count me in. I think my followers would love some tips on staying safe online. Plus, it would give me a chance to show that there's more to life than just filters and hashtags."

Together, they began brainstorming ideas, each adding their unique perspective on how they could make online security accessible and exciting. Aarushi's technical skills, Sophia's legal knowledge, and Kaneera's social media savvy created the perfect combination. The threat of the hacker had been a terrifying experience, but it also presented them with an opportunity to turn that fear into something powerful and proactive.

Taking Back Control Together

As they wrapped up the night, Aarushi closed her laptop, feeling a profound sense of accomplishment and relief. They had not only overcome a formidable challenge but had also empowered themselves in the process. The hacker might have tried to strip them of their privacy, but he had instead sparked a fire in them-a resolve to educate and protect others.

From that night on, they knew they weren't just users of the digital world; they were guardians of it, ready to face whatever new challenges might arise. Together, they had reclaimed their control, their security, and their sense of purpose.

For Aarushi, Kaneera, and Sophia, this was the beginning of a new journey. They had entered the digital world as individuals but emerged as a team, determined to make a difference in a world where many still walked unprotected.

9.2 Explaining Account Recovery, Data Protection, and How to Undo Damage

After successfully confronting the hacker, Aarushi, Sophia, and Kaneera sat back, reflecting on what they had just accomplished. Their digital lives had been invaded, and each of them felt the weight of having their private information exposed. They realized that while they had taken control back from the attacker, the process of fully restoring and securing their digital presence was only beginning. Aarushi led them through the steps to secure their accounts and repair the damage, making sure they fully understood the process of reclaiming privacy and control.

"Recovering an account isn't just about resetting a password," Aarushi began, pulling out her notes. "It's a full process that requires thorough checking, adding extra security layers, and knowing exactly what needs to be protected."

Kaneera was stunned, still visibly shaken by the invasion of her personal accounts. "I had no idea how deep these things go. I thought a quick password change was enough."

"Let's make sure you're fully protected this time," Aarushi said with a reassuring smile. "We'll go over everything."

RESTORING ACCESS TO Compromised Accounts

The first step in regaining control after a security breach is to recover access to any compromised accounts. Aarushi explained that it's crucial to identify all the accounts that may have been affected.

"Start with your email," Aarushi advised, "since it's the gateway to most of your other accounts. If someone has access to your email, they can use it to reset passwords on other accounts."

Aarushi guided Kaneera through verifying her email, checking recent login activity, and looking for any unfamiliar devices. They also enabled two-factor authentication (2FA), a security measure that requires both a password and a second verification step, usually a text message or authenticator app.

"When you add 2FA, it makes it harder for anyone to get in, even if they somehow get your password," Aarushi explained.

They followed the same process for Kaneera's social media accounts. Aarushi had Kaneera look over any connected apps or third-party services that had access to her profiles. "Sometimes hackers use these connected apps to get in without needing your actual login details," she said, encouraging Kaneera to remove any apps she no longer used or didn't recognize.

Sophia, watching carefully, took notes to implement these changes on her own accounts later. "It's like you have to fortify everything," she noted. "One weak link could bring the whole thing down."

Assessing and Controlling Data Exposure

Once they secured the accounts, Aarushi focused on the data exposure. "Even if you recover your accounts, you still need to think about the data that was stolen. What information did the hacker have access to? Were there any personal photos, messages, or documents?"

Kaneera looked uncomfortable, realizing just how much of her personal life had been laid bare. Aarushi reassured her, explaining how to go about damage control.

"First, make a list of anything sensitive or personal that was on your accounts," Aarushi said. "Think about direct messages, photos, or personal details like your address or phone number. Knowing what's exposed helps you control any fallout."

For Kaneera, this meant going through her social media account to delete any overly personal posts or messages. Aarushi also recommended Kaneera update her privacy settings to limit who could view her content. "This way, you reduce the chance of anyone outside your immediate network accessing your information."

They talked about protecting personal data beyond social media. Aarushi encouraged them to look at financial accounts, especially if any sensitive information had been compromised. "Check for any recent activity on your bank accounts, too, especially if your email or other identifying information was breached," Aarushi advised. "You might even consider freezing your credit temporarily if you think your personal data could be at risk."

Rebuilding Digital Privacy with Data Protection Tools

With their accounts secure and exposure assessed, Aarushi turned to data protection tools to add additional layers of security.

"You want to think of data protection as a continuous process," Aarushi said. "It's like having a security system in your home. Once you install it, you still need to do routine checks to make sure it's working."

She introduced Kaneera and Sophia to password managers, explaining that they securely store all passwords and help create stronger, unique ones for each account. "A password manager keeps everything in one place, and you only need to remember one master password. It's a lot safer than reusing the same password everywhere."

Aarushi also walked them through enabling backups for important files and data. She explained that a secure backup, whether on an encrypted external drive or a trusted cloud service, acts as a failsafe in case of future attacks. "With a backup, even if you get locked out, or your data gets erased, you have a safe copy of everything important."

Additionally, she suggested using a virtual private network (VPN) whenever accessing accounts on public Wi-Fi. "VPNs protect your connection by encrypting your data, so even if someone is snooping on the network, they won't be able to see what you're doing."

Kaneera downloaded a VPN on the spot, surprised by how straightforward it was. "I always thought these things were complicated, but this is actually pretty easy."

Strengthening Security with Regular Audits and Checks

Aarushi emphasized that digital security doesn't end once accounts are recovered. Regular audits and checks are necessary to prevent future incidents.

"Think of it like spring cleaning," Aarushi explained. "Every few months, go through your accounts, check your settings, and update your passwords. It keeps things tidy and secure."

Sophia suggested keeping a checklist of security practices, like reviewing 2FA settings, updating passwords, and checking for any suspicious activity. "Having it written down makes it easier to remember," she said, making a note in her journal.

Aarushi nodded, adding, "Also, be careful with the apps and services you link to your accounts. Some of them may have weaker security practices, so it's best to remove access for apps you don't actively use."

Together, they created a online security routine to revisit their privacy settings, review account access, and assess any new threats that could arise. Aarushi encouraged them to make it part of their digital habits, like checking email or updating their social media feeds.

Undoing Potential Damage with Professional Help and Reporting

Finally, Aarushi stressed that while they had managed to regain control on their own, some cases might require professional assistance. She explained how to report incidents to online security professionals or even legal authorities.

"If the damage is extensive, you might need help from a online security expert to remove advanced malware or repair compromised systems," she said. "And don't hesitate to report serious incidents to law enforcement, especially if there are threats involved."

Sophia, being in law, mentioned her interest in digital rights and privacy laws. "I think a lot of people don't realize they have options. They assume that if they're hacked, they're on their own."

Aarushi nodded in agreement, adding, "And hackers rely on that. They assume their victims won't know where to turn, which makes it easier for them to keep getting away with it."

They discussed how to gather evidence, such as screenshots and log files, to document any potential abuse or threats. Aarushi stressed that these records could be essential for both reporting incidents and strengthening legal cases if needed.

Moving Forward Stronger and Wiser

By the end of the night, Kaneera, Sophia, and Aarushi had not only regained control of their accounts and protected their data but had also armed themselves with the knowledge to prevent future attacks. Each of them had a new perspective on the importance of online security, privacy, and data protection.

"This experience taught us so much more than just protecting our accounts," Sophia remarked thoughtfully. "It's about understanding that we have control over our online presence-and we have the power to protect it."

Aarushi smiled, feeling proud of how far they had all come. "Exactly. And now, we're in a better position to help others protect themselves, too."

Together, they knew this journey wasn't just about fighting one hacker; it was a lasting lesson in resilience and vigilance. With every security layer they added, they were not only protecting themselves but inspiring each other to be proactive digital citizens, ready for whatever challenges might come next.

9.3 Kaneera Regains her Online Presence and Fights Back Against False Information

With their accounts restored and their data protected, Kaneera, Aarushi, and Sophia were beginning to feel a sense of normalcy return. Yet, for Kaneera, something still remained. Her online presence-the reputation she had worked so hard to build-had been damaged, twisted by false information and malicious rumors spread by the hacker. She knew she couldn't fully move forward until she addressed the misinformation head-on.

"Everything I've worked for feels tarnished now," Kaneera confided, scrolling through her account. Her followers were there, but engagement had dropped. Some had sent concerned messages, while others had distanced themselves due to the rumors that had spread.

Aarushi, who was working on her laptop beside Kaneera, looked up. "Kaneera, you've been through a lot. But we can fix this. Let's take back your narrative."

Kaneera nodded, determined. "I'm ready to fight back."

Reclaiming Control and Rebuilding Confidence

Kaneera's first step was regaining her confidence. The hacker had damaged her online reputation and shaken her sense of control over her image. She decided to take a positive stance, using her experience as a learning moment not only for herself but also for her followers.

"I want people to understand that no one's immune to this kind of attack," Kaneera explained. "If I can be targeted, anyone can. But instead of letting this define me, I'm going to use it as a platform to educate and help others."

Sophia, inspired by Kaneera's strength, offered her support. "Kaneera, that's powerful. Your story can turn this entire situation around."

Aarushi suggested they start with a new post-a message that directly addressed what had happened. "Let's take control by being transparent. You'll show your followers that you have nothing to hide."

Kaneera nodded, a spark of excitement returning to her eyes. "If I own this story, it won't belong to anyone else."

Crafting a Public Statement and Addressing the Rumors

Together, they crafted a heartfelt message for Kaneera's followers. In her post, Kaneera explained what had happened and expressed her gratitude for the support she had received from those who had stayed with her through the ordeal. She chose her words carefully, striking a balance between vulnerability and empowerment.

"Hey, everyone," she began, her fingers flowing over the keyboard, "I want to talk about something difficult that I've been going through recently. You may have noticed that I've been a bit quieter than usual, and there's a reason for that. My account was hacked, and it's been a challenging journey to reclaim it. But this experience has taught me so much about online safety, resilience, and the importance of protecting ourselves in the digital world."

She continued, addressing some of the rumors that had circulated about her. Instead of refuting each specific claim, Kaneera emphasized the importance of critical thinking and not believing everything online at face value. She encouraged her followers to question information and be mindful of potential misinformation.

"Social media can be a wonderful place, but it also has its dark sides," she wrote. "This experience has shown me how quickly false information can spread, and I want to encourage everyone to take a step back, think critically, and always prioritize kindness."

After a final read-through, Kaneera hit "Post." Almost instantly, messages of support and empathy began pouring in. Her followers expressed relief, understanding, and admiration for her strength. It was a decisive moment of reconnection and a reminder of the community she had built.

Enlisting the Help of Digital Allies

Kaneera knew that a single post wouldn't undo all the damage, but it was a start. To rebuild her presence further, Aarushi suggested reaching out to trusted influencers and online communities who could help her amplify her story and counteract the negative narratives.

"Think of it like creating a support network," Aarushi explained. "These are people who respect and trust you. By sharing your story, they can help spread the truth."

Kaneera reached out to a few fellow influencers and online friends, explaining what had happened and asking if they would help her get her story out. Each of them responded with overwhelming support, reposting her message and sharing their own words of encouragement.

These collaborations introduced her story to a broader audience and added credibility to her message. People who may have been skeptical were now seeing respected voices in the community standing behind her.

Combatting the Misinformation and Amplifying Positive Content

To further dilute the effect of false information, Kaneera, Aarushi, and Sophia developed a strategy to push positive content. Kaneera started posting more frequently, sharing genuine moments from her life, her passions, and her journey to reclaim her sense of security.

"I'm going to show them the real me," she said confidently. "I won't let that hacker's narrative be the last word."

She created a content schedule, balancing posts about her interests, collaborations with other creators, and educational pieces about online safety. Aarushi and Sophia suggested using hashtags that promoted digital awareness, which attracted new followers who appreciated her openness about online security and resilience.

Kaneera's audience started engaging more actively. Her positive, uplifting posts were shared widely, reaching beyond her usual followers. Over time, this influx of authentic content began to overshadow the remnants of the misinformation.

Securing Her Brand and Setting Boundaries

With her account steadily rebuilding, Kaneera decided it was time to establish firmer boundaries around her digital presence. Aarushi helped her set up security features that would further protect her brand and ensure a solid defense against any future threats.

They enabled additional layers of security on all her devices, adding 2FA to every connected account, setting up stronger passwords, and using a password manager to prevent weak or reused passwords. Aarushi also helped her create an alert system to monitor any unusual login activity.

"From now on, you'll have a much clearer view of who's accessing your accounts and when," Aarushi assured her. "If anything suspicious happens, you'll know right away."

Additionally, Kaneera established personal boundaries about the types of information she would share. She decided to avoid posting real-time updates about her location and reduced the amount of personal detail in her posts.

"This experience taught me a lot about the value of privacy," she said. "I can still be open with my followers, but I'll be more careful about protecting certain parts of my life."

Educating Her Followers and Creating Lasting Impact

As Kaneera continued to rebuild her online presence, she realized that her story had the power to make a lasting impact. She felt a new responsibility to educate her followers about online safety, and she started creating posts and stories focused on practical online security tips.

Her followers were receptive, engaging with her content and asking questions about how they could protect themselves online. Kaneera even hosted a live Q&A session with Aarushi, where they discussed online security basics, password strength, and the importance of using verified apps and secure networks.

"I feel like I'm finally in control again," Kaneera said after the session. "And it feels amazing to know I'm helping others protect themselves, too."

She even considered starting a new segment in her content called "Stay Safe Sundays," where she would share weekly tips and tricks on online safety. It became a place where her followers could ask questions and learn more about digital security, transforming her account into a source of positivity and empowerment.

Celebrating the Victory and Moving Forward

With her reputation restored and her following stronger than ever, Kaneera felt a renewed sense of purpose. She had taken back control, turning a traumatic experience into a journey of empowerment and resilience.

One evening, as the three friends celebrated their victory, Kaneera reflected on how far they had come. "I never thought I'd be able to turn this around, but thanks to both of you, I feel stronger than ever."

Sophia raised a toast. "To taking back control and helping others do the same."

Aarushi added with a smile, "And to being smarter, safer, and a lot more cautious online."

Kaneera's experience served as a reminder to her followers and friends alike that reclaiming control over one's online presence is possible, even after a significant breach. Her journey inspired others to prioritize digital safety and underscored the importance of resilience in the face of online threats.

In the end, Kaneera's story became more than just a lesson in online security-it was a testament to friendship, strength, and the power of owning one's narrative. And as the three friends continued their digital journey together, they knew they were more equipped than ever to face whatever the digital world might throw their way.

Chapter 10: Lessons Learned

10.1 The Aftermath: Rebuilding Online Security and Protecting Personal Data

In the weeks following their confrontation with the cybercriminal, Aarushi, Kaneera, and Sophia found themselves reflecting on everything they had gone through. The threats, the invasion of privacy, the loss of control-all of it had forced them to reconsider their online lives and make fundamental changes in how they approached security and privacy.

THE THREE FRIENDS REALIZED that their journey wasn't just about recovering from an attack; it was about rebuilding their online presence with a newfound strength and awareness of the importance of protecting personal data. The experience had left a mark on them, but it also inspired a commitment to protect themselves and others from similar threats.

Rebuilding Security from the Ground Up

After the cybercriminal was exposed and the threat neutralized, Aarushi encouraged Kaneera and Sophia to go beyond the immediate security measures they'd implemented. They needed to build a more secure digital presence from the ground up, starting with the basics they had initially overlooked.

Reassessing Security Protocols

Aarushi explained that rebuilding online security started with understanding and re-evaluating their entire digital ecosystem. "It's not enough to just have a strong password or enable two-factor authentication," she said. "We need to review everything-our devices, our accounts, and even our daily habits."

They began by updating passwords across all accounts and implementing unique, complex passwords for each one. Aarushi also introduced Kaneera and Sophia to a password manager, which generated strong passwords and stored them securely. This would allow them to have distinct passwords without the worry of forgetting them.

Implementing Multi-Layered Security

In addition to strengthening passwords, Aarushi showed them how to add layers to their online security. They enabled two-factor authentication (2FA) on every account that supported it, using authentication apps rather than SMS where possible, as SMS verification can be vulnerable to SIM-swapping attacks.

"Think of it like locking both the front and back doors, plus setting an alarm system," Aarushi explained. "The more layers we add, the harder it is for anyone to break in."

They also reviewed their devices and accounts for unused apps and old, forgotten accounts, removing anything that could be a potential vulnerability. "Every app, every account is an entry point," Aarushi reminded them. "If we're not using it, it's best to remove it."

Protecting Personal Data Going Forward

A key takeaway from their ordeal was understanding just how much personal data they shared online, often without even realizing it. The cybercriminals had exploited even the smallest bits of information, piecing together their lives in ways they hadn't anticipated.

Limiting Information Shared Online

Kaneera, in particular, found herself rethinking how she approached her social media presence. She realized that while her openness had helped her connect with her followers, it had also made her vulnerable. Aarushi and Sophia helped her create a set of guidelines for sharing content.

"From now on," Kaneera decided, "I'll avoid posting real-time locations, reduce personal details, and think carefully about what I'm sharing."

She began filtering her posts, removing or archiving older content that contained too much personal information. For new posts, she committed to keeping sensitive details private and began using privacy features on her social media platforms to control who could see her content.

Sophia also began to limit her digital footprint. As a law student, she knew that privacy was a fundamental right, and she started taking steps to protect her own data. She reviewed privacy settings across her accounts and even used alias emails for non-essential sign-ups to reduce the exposure of her personal information.

Controlling Digital Footprints

Aarushi reminded her friends that controlling their digital footprint meant being vigilant about what they allowed others to access. She helped Kaneera and Sophia set up alerts for any unusual online activity, such as unauthorized login attempts, and taught them how to check for data breaches involving their accounts. They registered with services that could notify them if any of their personal information was found in a data breach, enabling them to take quick action if needed.

Creating a New Digital Awareness

After the initial steps of rebuilding their security, the trio began looking at their experience as a stepping stone to educating others. They realized that many people might not understand the extent of digital risks or how to protect themselves, so they decided to share their insights and lessons learned.

Building Awareness in Their Communities

Kaneera, with Aarushi and Sophia's help, began incorporating online safety tips into her social media content. Her experience had created a new purpose for her platform-she wanted to use her voice to educate her followers about the importance of online security and digital privacy.

"People need to know that these threats are real," Kaneera explained. "If my story can help even one person avoid what I went through, it's worth it."

Sophia reached out to her law school network to discuss the implications of online threats on privacy rights. She organized an online seminar where she and Aarushi shared their experiences, offered practical advice on securing digital information, and discussed the legal aspects of online threats.

Their efforts created a ripple effect, sparking conversations about digital privacy within their communities and prompting others to take their own security seriously.

Reinforcing Trust and Accountability

Throughout their journey, one of the most profound lessons they learned was about trust-who to trust with their information and how to rebuild that trust when it was broken.

Practicing Caution with Third-Party Apps and Platforms

Aarushi emphasized the importance of being selective with third-party apps and platforms, as they can often be the weakest links in security. The friends reviewed the permissions granted to each app on their devices, removing those that requested excessive access to personal information or offered questionable value.

"Not every app deserves to know everything about us," Aarushi explained. "It's about being cautious and only granting access where it's truly necessary."

They learned to research any app or platform before using it, reading reviews, checking permissions, and ensuring it came from reputable sources. Trust, they realized, had to be earned-especially in the digital world.

Establishing a Regular Security Routine

Rebuilding security wasn't a one-time effort; it was an ongoing commitment. Aarushi encouraged Kaneera and Sophia to adopt regular security checkups. They set a routine to review and update passwords, check account activity, and verify that their security settings were up to date.

"This is like doing maintenance on your car," Aarushi said. "A little attention now can save you a lot of trouble down the road."

They also decided to hold each other accountable, reminding one another to adhere to their security routines and sharing any new insights or threats they encountered.

Moving Forward with Strength and Awareness

As they completed their journey of rebuilding and strengthening their online security, the friends reflected on how far they had come. The experience not only taught them practical skills but also reshaped their mindset about the digital world.

For Kaneera, it meant balancing her love for social media with a commitment to personal security. For Sophia, it reinforced her drive to protect privacy rights and gave her a deeper understanding of the personal impact of online threats. And for Aarushi, it reaffirmed her passion for helping others navigate the complex landscape of online security.

Embracing a New Level of Confidence and Caution

The ordeal had been difficult, but it left them stronger and more aware. They learned that while the digital world holds incredible possibilities, it also requires a sense of caution and responsibility.

"We may not be able to control everything," Aarushi said one evening as they reflected on their journey, "but we can control how we approach it. We've taken back our power, and that's what matters."

They shared a sense of accomplishment, knowing that they had emerged from a challenging experience with new knowledge, resilience, and the determination to protect themselves and others.

A New Chapter: Advocating for Digital Safety

With a renewed sense of purpose, the trio began brainstorming ways to continue their advocacy for digital safety. They discussed creating an online group dedicated to sharing online security tips and personal stories, a space where others could feel supported and educated about their own online security.

Through their combined efforts, they aimed to foster a community that understood the importance of digital privacy, and they felt confident that their experiences could make a difference. The challenges they had faced had shown them just how interconnected the online world was and how, by supporting one another, they could build a safer digital environment.

As they moved forward, Aarushi, Kaneera, and Sophia knew that their story was far from over. But they were ready for whatever came next, armed with the knowledge, strength, and unity that had carried them through their journey.

In taking control of their digital lives, they had become more than just survivors of an online attack; they had become advocates, protectors, and leaders in the movement for digital safety and personal empowerment. In this new chapter of their lives, they knew they would continue to make a positive impact-one secure step at a time.

10.2 Reflecting on What They Learned and How Others can Protect Themselves

In the aftermath of their harrowing journey through the maze of online threats, Aarushi, Kaneera, and Sophia found themselves looking back on the lessons learned. The experience had been a whirlwind, but it had equipped them with invaluable knowledge-not only about online security but also about resilience, trust, and responsibility in the digital world.

Each friend took time to reflect on what they'd learned, hoping that others could benefit from their insights. They knew that sharing these lessons could help protect others from facing similar threats, empowering people to take charge of their digital security and navigate the online world with confidence.

LESSON 1: RECOGNIZING the Scope of Online threats

One of the trio's biggest realizations was the sheer scale of potential online threats. It was no longer a question of "if" but "when" a person might encounter online risks. They realized that anyone could be a target, regardless of how "ordinary" their online presence might seem.

Reflecting on this, Aarushi noted, “Online threats are constantly evolving. It’s important to stay informed so you’re never caught off guard. We’re all potential targets, but with the right knowledge, we can turn ourselves into difficult ones.”

For Kaneera, this new awareness meant understanding how her social media presence could attract unwanted attention. “I’ve learned that we can’t assume everyone who follows us has good intentions,” she said. “Being aware of who’s watching is the first step in protecting ourselves.”

Sophia, too, gained perspective on the scope of online threats from her legal perspective. She recognized that the laws protecting digital privacy were still catching up with the speed of technological advancement. “The more informed we are, the more empowered we are to navigate these vulnerabilities until stronger policies are in place," she concluded.

Lesson 2: The Importance of Basic Cyber Hygiene

During their journey, the friends realized how foundational practices like having strong passwords, using two-factor authentication, and keeping software up-to-date could significantly improve their protection against common online attacks.

"Cyber hygiene is like personal hygiene," Aarushi explained. "You might not see the germs or viruses right away, but they're there. Keeping your devices and accounts secure is the digital version of washing your hands-simple, but it can prevent a lot of harm."

Kaneera admitted that she'd never paid much attention to the strength of her passwords or even considered using a password manager. "I used to think it was too much trouble," she said, laughing at her former self. "But after what I went through, I realize it's so much easier than dealing with a hacked account."

The friends discussed how critical it was to start with these basic practices and maintain them as part of their daily routines. They hoped that by sharing this knowledge, they could help others see how easy and essential it was to implement these practices.

Lesson 3: Staying Vigilant Against Social Engineering

One of the most eye-opening moments for the friends was understanding how much information could be manipulated and used against them. They learned that online attacks weren't just about complex codes or technical exploits-they often involved manipulation, deception, and gaining trust through social engineering.

Sophia reflected on this with a sense of urgency. "Social engineering is everywhere, and it's often disguised as something harmless. Recognizing these tricks is crucial to protecting ourselves."

Aarushi reminded her friends to be cautious about sharing personal details with strangers or even acquaintances online. "Cyber criminals rely on familiarity. They want you to let your guard down.

Staying vigilant doesn't mean being paranoid; it means knowing when to be cautious."

They discussed simple but effective strategies, like avoiding oversharing on social media, double-checking the legitimacy of emails, and thinking twice before clicking on unfamiliar links. Aarushi encouraged everyone to question the motives of people they interacted with online, reminding them that a bit of doubt could go a long way in preventing social engineering attacks.

Lesson 4: Empowering Yourself with Knowledge

As they recounted their experiences, the friends realized that knowledge was their greatest weapon. The more they understood about online security, the better equipped they were to spot potential threats and take proactive measures.

"Learning about online security is like learning self-defense," Aarushi said. "The more you know, the more confident you become in protecting yourself."

Sophia took this lesson to heart, diving deeper into privacy laws and digital rights. She became an advocate for personal privacy, educating others about the importance of protecting their information. "We have a right to privacy," she said. "And knowing our rights empowers us to defend them."

Kaneera began sharing what she had learned with her followers, encouraging them to prioritize their online safety. "I want my followers to know they don't have to be experts in tech to protect themselves," she said. "They just need to understand a few key things and be willing to act on them."

Lesson 5: Building a Support System and Sharing Experiences

One of the most valuable takeaways from their journey was the importance of having a support system. Facing online threats alone could be overwhelming, but together, the friends found the strength and motivation to tackle each challenge.

"Having each other made all the difference," Kaneera said. "I know I wouldn't have been able to handle it on my own. There's power in sharing our experiences and learning together."

Aarushi agreed, emphasizing that no one should feel ashamed or embarrassed about seeking help if they experience cyber harassment or other online threats. "Online security isn't just about protecting yourself; it's about supporting others. When we share our experiences, we make it easier for others to come forward and find solutions."

Together, they decided to create an online support group where people could discuss their own online security experiences and learn from one another. They believed that creating a safe space for others to share their stories would help more people understand the importance of online security and empower them to take control of their digital lives.

Practical Tips for Everyday Online security

With a commitment to help others, the friends compiled a list of practical tips to guide those who wanted to protect their digital lives. They hoped these tips would empower readers to take small but effective steps toward enhancing their online security.

1. **Use Strong, Unique Passwords:** Avoid using the same password across multiple accounts, and make sure each password is complex and difficult to guess. Consider using a password manager to keep track of them securely.

2. **Enable Two-Factor Authentication (2FA):** Whenever possible, add a layer of security by enabling 2FA on your accounts. This helps protect against unauthorized access, even if someone knows your password.

3. **Be Cautious of Suspicious Links and Emails:** Avoid clicking on links or downloading attachments from unknown sources. Phishing emails and malicious links are common tactics used by cybercriminals to steal information.

4. **Limit Personal Information Shared Online:** Think carefully about what you post on social media, especially details about your location, schedule, or personal life. Cybercriminals can use this information to target you.

5. **Regularly Update Software and Apps:** Keep your devices and apps updated to ensure they have the latest security patches. Outdated software can have vulnerabilities that cybercriminals exploit.

6. **Monitor Accounts for Unusual Activity:** Review your accounts regularly for suspicious activity, such as unfamiliar logins or changes to account settings if your accounts offer this feature, set up notifications for unusual activity.

7. **Use Encryption Tools:** For sensitive files and communications, use encryption tools to protect your data. This adds an extra layer of security, especially for personal or financial information.

8. **Avoid Public Wi-Fi for Sensitive Transactions:** Public Wi-Fi networks are often unsecured, making it easy for cybercriminals to intercept data. If you need to use public Wi-Fi, consider using a VPN to secure your connection.

9. Regularly Back Up Important Data: Regular backups ensure that you don't lose important files if your device is compromised. Store backups in secure, offline locations.

10. Educate Yourself Continuously: Online threats are constantly evolving, so staying informed about new risks and security measures is essential. Follow trusted sources, attend webinars, and engage with online communities to keep up-to-date.

Moving Forward with Confidence and Preparedness

As the friends shared their reflections, they felt a renewed sense of purpose and confidence. They knew that they couldn't control every aspect of the digital world, but they could control how they approached it. Their journey had empowered them, and they were ready to face whatever came next with a blend of caution, resilience, and knowledge.

Aarushi, Kaneera, and Sophia hoped that by sharing their story, others would feel inspired to take their online safety seriously. They wanted people to know that they didn't have to be tech experts to protect themselves and that small actions could make a big difference.

In the end, they learned that online security was about more than just technology-it was about safeguarding their identities, their connections, and their peace of mind. And as they moved forward, they were determined to continue spreading this message, ensuring that everyone could feel safe and secure in the digital world.

With a sense of unity and a drive to protect others, Aarushi, Kaneera, and Sophia embarked on a new chapter, using the lessons they'd learned to help others and build a community of digitally empowered individuals. They knew that online security was a journey, not a destination, and they were ready to walk that path-together.

10.3 Best Practices for Long-Term Online Security

As Aarushi, Kaneera, and Sophia reflected on their journey, they recognized that online security wasn't just about short-term fixes; it required a commitment to long-term practices. Staying safe online meant developing habits that would protect them not only in the present but also in the future. Here, they outlined essential practices anyone could adopt to ensure sustained digital security, covering practical tips for keeping personal information secure while navigating the ever-changing online landscape.

Regularly Update Passwords and Use Unique Ones for Each Account

Aarushi was quick to emphasize that strong, unique passwords are the first line of defense against unauthorized access. She explained that even a single weak or repeated password could be the key a hacker needs to access multiple accounts.

Tips for Password Security:

- Use a password manager to generate and store strong, unique passwords for each account.
- Change passwords regularly-especially for sensitive accounts like banking or email.
- Enable two-factor authentication (2FA) whenever possible for an added layer of security, which will help safeguard accounts even if a password is compromised.
- Educate Yourself on Emerging Threats and Scams

Sophia's legal background reminded her of the importance of staying informed about the ever-evolving tactics that cybercriminals use. She pointed out that just as traditional scams have evolved, online threats continuously adapt to new technologies and user behaviors.

Steps to Stay Updated:

- Follow reliable online security blogs and news sources to keep up with emerging threats.
- Participate in workshops, webinars, or online courses focused on online security basics.
- Subscribe to alerts from reputable organizations like the online security and Infrastructure Security Agency (CISA), which publishes up-to-date information on threats and preventative measures.

Monitor and Limit the Information You Share Online

Kaneera's experiences with social media taught her the importance of being mindful of the information she shared online. She noted that while sharing personal moments was enjoyable, it was crucial to draw boundaries and be cautious of oversharing.

Tips for Information Control:

- Review privacy settings on all social media accounts to control who can see your posts.
- Be selective with location sharing and disable it where possible, especially on social platforms.
- Limit personal information in public profiles and posts, and avoid sharing details like your full birthdate, address, or daily routines.

Secure All Devices and Regularly Update Software

Aarushi pointed out that securing their personal devices was essential, as malware and spyware often target outdated systems. She emphasized that installing updates and patches was a simple but effective way to keep systems protected from known vulnerabilities.

Device Security Tips:

- Enable automatic updates on all devices, including smartphones, tablets, and computers.
- Install a reputable antivirus and anti-malware program, and run regular scans.
- Keep firewalls enabled on computers and routers to provide an additional layer of protection.
- Avoid downloading software or apps from unverified sources, as they could contain malware.

Use VPNs and Secure Networks, Especially on Public Wi-Fi

Sophia reminded her friends of the dangers of public Wi-Fi, where cybercriminals often wait to intercept data on unsecured networks. Using a Virtual Private Network (VPN) was an effective way to stay secure, especially when accessing sensitive information.

Best Practices for Network Security:

- Use a VPN on public Wi-Fi to encrypt internet traffic and protect data from potential eavesdroppers.
- Avoid conducting sensitive transactions, like online banking, while on public Wi-Fi.
- Ensure that home Wi-Fi networks are secured with strong passwords

and use WPA3 encryption if available.

Regularly Review Account Activity and Set up Alerts

Monitoring account activity is a proactive way to detect unusual behavior early. Kaneera learned this lesson the hard way, but she now understood how helpful it was to stay vigilant and receive notifications on any suspicious activity.

Steps for Account Monitoring:

- Set up email or text alerts for any unusual login attempts or suspicious transactions.
- Regularly review your account's login history on social media and financial accounts.
- Periodically check financial statements for unfamiliar charges or transactions.

Practice Safe Browsing and Be Wary of Phishing Attempts

Aarushi underscored the importance of staying cautious while browsing the internet. She explained how phishing attacks and suspicious links were often used to trick people into providing sensitive information or installing malware.

Tips for Safe Browsing:

- Be cautious about clicking on unfamiliar links or downloading attachments from unknown senders.
- Verify the legitimacy of URLs and look for signs of secure sites (like "https" and a padlock icon).
- Don't enter personal information on websites unless you're sure of their authenticity.

Back-Up Important Data Regularly

Sophia highlighted the importance of data backups, pointing out that losing access to important files due to cyber threats like ransomware could be devastating. A reliable backup plan could prevent data loss and provide peace of mind.

Data Backup Tips:

- Back up important files to external hard drives or secure cloud storage services.
- Schedule automatic backups to ensure data is always current.
- Keep at least one copy of backups offline to protect against ransomware that targets networked devices.

Be Cautious with Apps and Browser Extensions

Aarushi explained that apps and browser extensions could sometimes serve as entry points for malware and spyware. She stressed the importance of downloading only reputable apps and extensions and reviewing their permissions.

App and Extension Safety Tips:

- Download apps only from official app stores like Google Play or the Apple App Store.
- Review permissions before installing any app or extension-ensure they only access what's necessary for functionality.
- Periodically audit and delete unused apps or extensions that may be gathering data unnecessarily.

Maintain a Healthy Skepticism Online

Lastly, Sophia encouraged her friends to maintain a healthy level of skepticism in their digital interactions. With the increase in social engineering tactics, staying vigilant about requests for personal information was more important than ever.

Tips for Online Skepticism:

- Be wary of unsolicited requests for personal or financial information, especially over email or text.
- Avoid sharing personal details with people you don't know or trust, even if they seem friendly or familiar.
- If something seems too good to be true-whether a job offer, a financial opportunity, or an exciting prize-verify its legitimacy before taking

action.

Integrating online security into Daily Life

The friends realized that the key to long-term online security was to incorporate these practices into their daily routines. Online security wasn't a one-time effort; it was an ongoing process that required consistency and vigilance. By turning these steps into habits, they could navigate the digital world with greater confidence and security.

Reflecting on their journey, Aarushi, Kaneera, and Sophia hoped to inspire others to approach online security as an essential aspect of modern life. The threats they had faced were real, but so were the tools and strategies available to combat them.

The Final Takeaway: Empowerment through Knowledge and Action

For the trio, the biggest lesson was that online security wasn't just about protection-it was about empowerment. By understanding the risks and taking proactive measures, they felt in control of their digital lives. They knew they weren't invincible, but they were no longer helpless. They had transformed from unaware users to informed digital citizens.

Aarushi shared a final piece of advice: "Remember that online security is a journey, not a destination. Stay informed, stay cautious, and never be afraid to ask questions. The more you know, the better equipped you'll be to protect yourself and those around you."

Kaneera and Sophia echoed her sentiment, agreeing that the journey had changed them for the better. They had not only protected themselves but had become advocates for online safety, ready to share their newfound knowledge with others.

In the end, their story was about more than just neutralizing a cybercriminal. It was a journey of self-discovery, resilience, and empowerment-proving that with knowledge, determination, and support, anyone could take control of their digital world. Together, they had unlocked the tools needed to protect their digital lives, and they were ready to step confidently into the future, knowing they had the skills to handle whatever came next.

Chapter 11: Online Security for Everyone

11.1 Expanding the Message: Kaneera Starts a Campaign on Social Media to Raise Online Security Awareness

With the ordeal behind them, Kaneera, Aarushi, and Sophia found themselves reflecting on their experience. They had all learned so much about online security, online privacy, and the exposures that come with a connected lifestyle. For Kaneera, this experience had been a wake-up call-not just for herself but also for her followers, who might be steering similar digital threats without knowing it. Inspired by her new awareness and armed with insights from Aarushi and Sophia, Kaneera decided it was time to take action. She would use her influence to start a campaign on social media, aiming to empower others with the knowledge she had gained.

Sitting together in their favorite café, Kaneera shared her idea with Aarushi and Sophia.

"I want to start a campaign on online security," she said, her voice brimming with excitement. "There are so many people out there, especially young girls, who might be making the same mistakes I did. If we could get even a fraction of them to take online security seriously, think about the impact!"

Aarushi nodded, her expression thoughtful. "That's a brilliant idea. I've noticed that a lot of online security information out there is either too technical or just plain boring. But if you put it out in a way that people can relate to, it could actually make a difference."

Sophia leaned in, her legal mind already framing the practicalities. "We could structure it as a series. Start with the basics, like password protection, and then work up to more serious issues like phishing and account recovery. What do you think, Kaneera?"

Kaneera's eyes lit up. "Exactly! And maybe we could give each topic a catchy name, something that grabs attention. I could make short videos or infographics or even host live Q&As."

They brainstormed for hours, listing the topics they would cover and discussing ways to make each one accessible. As they sipped their coffees, Kaneera sketched out the beginnings of a campaign plan on her tablet, drawing from the very steps they had taken over the past months.

Crafting the Campaign: #StaySecure Series

Kaneera decided to name the campaign #StaySecure-a simple yet effective name. She wanted her followers to feel empowered, as though they could take control of their online lives with just a few straightforward actions. The goal was to make online security feel as approachable as skincare routines or fashion tips, breaking down the idea that digital security was only for tech experts.

The campaign would be divided into several themes, each focused on a specific aspect of online security:

- #PasswordPower – The importance of strong passwords and using two-factor authentication.
- #ThinkBeforeYouClick – Identifying and avoiding phishing attacks.
- #PrivacyPlease – Understanding privacy settings on social media.
- #DataDefense – Protecting personal information from being shared or sold.
- #SafeBrowsing – Staying safe on public Wi-Fi and avoiding sketchy websites.

The #StaySecure series would include a mix of posts, stories, and live videos. Each theme would highlight a real-life scenario or a relatable experience that Kaneera herself had faced, emphasizing that online security was relevant to everyone, not just tech-savvy individuals.

Kickstarting #PasswordPower

The first theme in the #StaySecure series, #PasswordPower, focused on the basics of creating strong passwords and the importance of two-factor authentication. Kaneera knew that many people still used passwords that were simple and easy to guess. So, she decided to start by sharing her own mistakes in a light-hearted way.

With Aarushi's guidance, Kaneera crafted a post about the importance of strong passwords, using examples that would resonate with her followers:

"#StaySecure: Who else used their dog's name as their password? I'll admit it-I used to think that was safe! But here's the truth: simple passwords make it way easier for hackers to get in. So, let's get creative with our passwords! Try to mix letters, numbers, and symbols, and keep it unique for every account. It may sound tricky, but trust me, once you start using a password manager, you'll never go back. "

She paired this post with a story about how her own account had been compromised and how changing her passwords had helped her feel more secure. Her followers responded enthusiastically, sharing their own experiences with weak passwords and asking for tips on using password managers. Many were surprised to learn how easy it was to improve their online security with just a few simple changes.

Sharing #ThinkBeforeYouClick

The next theme, #ThinkBeforeYouClick, addressed the dangers of phishing scams. With Aarushi's help, Kaneera crafted a short video showing common phishing tactics, including fake emails and links disguised as legitimate websites.

In the video, Kaneera explained, "Phishing attacks are like online traps. They look legit, but one wrong click, and your info could be in someone else's hands. If you're ever in doubt, don't click. Double-check, and ask yourself: does this link look right? Is the email address legit? Always be cautious."

The video quickly gained traction, with followers expressing how relatable and informative it was. Some even shared stories about times they'd almost fallen for similar scams. Kaneera encouraged them to share these experiences with the hashtag #ThinkBeforeYouClick, promoting a community of support where people could learn from each other's close calls and successes.

Addressing #PrivacyPlease

Privacy was a more sensitive topic, but Kaneera approached it with a mix of seriousness and warmth. She explained that understanding privacy settings was crucial, especially for influencers or anyone who shared a lot online.

For this post, Kaneera wrote, "#PrivacyPlease: Privacy isn't just a setting-it's a choice. Make sure you know who can see what on your profiles. Trust me, oversharing can invite the wrong kind of attention. Take a moment to review your settings on social media and think twice before sharing personal details."

Her followers responded positively, appreciating her openness and practical advice. By the time she finished the post, Kaneera felt she was genuinely making an impact. Many of her followers shared screenshots of their privacy settings, tagging her with notes of gratitude for the reminder.

Going Viral: The Impact of #StaySecure

As the campaign progressed, it gained unexpected momentum. People began tagging their friends, sharing the posts widely, and engaging in Kaneera's live Q&A sessions. She was thrilled to see her followers taking online security seriously, with many thanking her for bringing attention to such important issues in an accessible way.

Aarushi and Sophia watched Kaneera's campaign flourish with pride. They had all faced their challenges together, and now Kaneera was using her platform to spread the knowledge they'd gained. Aarushi was especially gratified to see more people talking about online safety without feeling overwhelmed or out of place.

One evening, after a particularly successful live Q&A, Kaneera received a message from a follower. It read, "Thank you, Kaneera! I've always felt like online security was way over my head, but you've made it feel like something I can actually understand and do. You've helped me feel safer online!"

After reading the message, Kaneera felt a deep sense of accomplishment. The #StaySecure campaign had started as a way to give back, but it had evolved into something much bigger-a movement that was helping others take control of their online safety.

The Ripple Effect

Kaneera's campaign didn't just stop with her followers. Soon, other influencers and digital creators started joining in, resharing Kaneera's posts and even creating their own content inspired by the #StaySecure series. A larger conversation about online safety was unfolding across social media, reaching people who might never have considered online security a priority.

Seeing this, Aarushi and Sophia encouraged Kaneera to take things even further. They suggested reaching out to local schools and organizations to offer workshops on online security. The campaign could extend beyond social media, allowing Kaneera to connect with people offline and provide hands-on guidance.

Kaneera embraced the idea, and with her friend's help, she began planning her first community workshop. The trio spent hours designing the curriculum, with Aarushi leading the tech demos, Sophia covering the legal side, and Kaneera sharing her personal journey.

Their first workshop was a resounding success, attracting attendees from all walks of life, from high school students to retirees. Each attendee left with a better understanding of how to protect themselves online and a newfound confidence in managing their digital lives.

Empowering Others: The Ultimate Victory

Through #StaySecure, Kaneera had gone from a social media influencer focused on lifestyle content to a powerful advocate for digital safety. By sharing her story and raising awareness; she empowered her followers to take control of their online security. But more importantly, she had shown them that protecting themselves online was within their reach, no matter their level of tech expertise.

Kaneera's journey had come full circle. What began as a personal challenge to overcome her own security vulnerabilities had evolved into a mission to educate and inspire others. As she looked at the growing #StaySecure community, she felt immense pride-not just in what she'd accomplished but in the people she had empowered along the way.

For Aarushi, Sophia, and Kaneera, the #StaySecure campaign was more than a project; it was a reminder of the strength they'd found in each other and the impact they could have when they joined forces. They knew that this was only the beginning of their journey, with more challenges and opportunities to make a difference awaiting them in the digital world.

11.2 Final Lessons on Protecting Privacy, Dealing with Threats, and Staying Safe Online

As the #StaySecure campaign took off, Aarushi, Kaneera, and Sophia decided it was time to share their most important takeaways on protecting privacy, handling threats, and staying safe in the online world. Each of them approached the topic from their unique perspective, bringing their own expertise and experiences to the conversation. They knew that, ultimately, digital safety wasn't just about following a list of rules-it was about cultivating habits and mindsets that would empower their followers to navigate the digital world confidently.

Gathered in a cozy coffee shop, the trio prepared a live video where they'd each offer their insights, hoping to reach as many people as possible with these final lessons. The video was set up in a casual, friendly style, with the three of them seated together, laughing and talking candidly, which resonated with their audience. Each had a different strength to share, and together, they presented a well-rounded view of online safety.

Aarushi's Lessons: Tech-Savvy Tools and Smarter Security

As the group's online security expert, Aarushi was the first to take the spotlight. She leaned in with her trademark warmth and clarity, explaining concepts that might otherwise feel intimidating.

"Let's start with a foundation," Aarushi began, her tone calm and welcoming. "Remember, your online privacy isn't just about what you're willing to share; it's also about what you're protecting from others. Think of the internet as a giant room full of people. Some are trustworthy, and some... well, not so much. You need to put up barriers to ensure only the right people get through."

Aarushi's first tip was about strong passwords. She reminded the audience of the importance of unique passwords for each account and recommended using a password manager to simplify the process. She explained, "Password managers are like secure vaults. They remember everything for you and keep it encrypted, so you don't have to worry about hackers guessing or cracking your passwords." She shared her own experiences, noting how using a password manager had given her peace of mind, especially with the dozens of accounts she managed.

Next, Aarushi introduced two-factor authentication (2FA), highlighting how it adds an extra layer of security. "Think of it as a double lock on your door. Even if someone somehow guesses your password, they still won't be able to get in without that second step." She demonstrated how to enable 2FA on popular platforms, walking viewers through the process step-by-step.

Aarushi also emphasized the importance of safe browsing habits. She urged people to be cautious on public Wi-Fi and to use virtual private networks (VPNs) to secure their connections. "A VPN is like an invisibility cloak," she explained with a smile. "It hides your online activity from potential eavesdroppers, which is especially important when you're on public networks, like in coffee shops or airports."

Wrapping up her portion, Aarushi encouraged her followers to be proactive about their online safety. "Security isn't something you do once and forget about. Make it a habit. Regularly update your passwords, check your privacy settings, and stay informed about new threats. With these tools and a little vigilance, you can protect yourself from most online risks."

Kaneera's Lessons: Protecting Privacy and Navigating Social Media Safely

When it was Kaneera's turn, she shared her unique perspective as a social media influencer. Kaneera's voice was empathetic, as she understood firsthand the challenges of balancing a public online presence with personal safety.

"Let's talk about privacy," Kaneera began, leaning forward as though she were sharing a secret. "Privacy isn't just about what you keep hidden; it's also about what you choose to share. I've learned that while being open online can be amazing, oversharing can sometimes attract the wrong kind of attention."

Her first piece of advice focused on setting boundaries with personal information. "Before you post, ask yourself: Do I want everyone to know this?

Or just close friends?" She demonstrated how to use privacy settings on various social media platforms to control who could see her posts, explaining that small adjustments like this could make a big difference in staying safe.

Kaneera also spoke about the importance of recognizing red flags online. "If someone you don't know is asking for personal information or pressuring you to share things you're uncomfortable with, trust your instincts and don't engage." She recounted her own experience with cyberstalking, emphasizing that it's okay to block or report suspicious accounts and to seek help if something feels off.

To add a personal touch, Kaneera shared a few specific strategies for protecting mental well-being online. She encouraged her followers to take breaks from social media when needed, avoid comparing themselves to others, and remember that their worth isn't defined by likes or followers. "Your mental health is just as important as your physical safety," she said with sincerity. "If anything online makes you feel uncomfortable or unsafe, take a step back."

Kaneera ended with a reminder to be cautious with location tags and check-ins. She explained how sharing her location in real-time had, at times, made her vulnerable to unwanted attention. "If you want to share a cool place you visited, consider posting about it later when you're no longer there. This way, you can enjoy the moment without worrying about who might be watching."

Sophia's Lessons: Understanding Legal Rights and reporting online Incidents

Sophia, the group's legal expert, rounded off their session by addressing the often-overlooked legal aspects of online security. Her insights were clear and empowering, meant to show viewers that they had rights and recourse in the face of digital threats.

"Let's talk about something people don't always think about your digital rights," Sophia began, her voice steady and reassuring. "No one has the right to invade your privacy or make you feel unsafe online. And if they do, there are legal steps you can take to protect yourself."

Sophia explained the concept of cyber harassment laws and how they're designed to protect individuals from online abuse, stalking, and intimidation. She shared specific examples of cases where victims had successfully taken legal action against perpetrators, emphasizing that online harassment was just as serious as offline harassment. "The internet may feel anonymous, but that doesn't mean people can do whatever they want without consequences. If someone crosses the line, you have options."

She walked through the process of reporting cyber incidents to law enforcement and online platforms. Sophia advised her audience to keep records of any abusive messages, screenshots, or emails as evidence. "Documentation is key. If something happens, save everything. This will help you make a stronger case if you decide to report it."

Sophia also stressed the importance of knowing your privacy rights and understanding how platforms handle personal data. "Most social media sites have terms of service that explain what they do with your data," she said. "Take a few minutes to review these settings and adjust them to your comfort level. Your data is valuable, and you have the right to decide how it's used."

Ending her segment, Sophia encouraged her viewers to speak up if they felt their rights were being violated. "Remember, you're not alone. If something feels wrong, talk to someone you trust or seek legal advice. There are people and resources out there that can help you reclaim your safety and peace of mind."

A United Front: The Three Friends' Message

As they wrapped up the live video, Aarushi, Kaneera, and Sophia took a moment to emphasize their shared message. Each friend had brought their own perspective-technical, personal, and legal-but together, they wanted to remind their audience that online security was for everyone.

Aarushi looked into the camera with a warm smile. "Remember, being safe online isn't about being paranoid; it's about being prepared. You have the power to protect yourself with just a few simple steps."

Kaneera nodded, chiming in, "And don't be afraid to set boundaries. Just because something is online doesn't mean it's any less real. Your safety matters, both in the physical world and online."

Sophia concluded with a firm yet reassuring tone. "Know your rights and stand up for them. No one has the right to make you feel unsafe. And if they try, remember that you have the law on your side."

As the live video ended, the three friends were met with an outpouring of gratitude from their followers. Many shared comments about feeling more informed and empowered, and some even pledged to take their first steps toward securing their digital lives. The three friends had set out to make a difference, and the impact was undeniable.

For Aarushi, Kaneera, and Sophia, this campaign wasn't just about spreading awareness; it was about giving their audience the tools to protect themselves and encouraging them to take control of their own online lives. Their message was clear: online security was within everyone's reach, and it started with a little knowledge, a few proactive steps, and a strong community.

11.3 Aarushi and Sophia Continue Their Journeys into Online Security and Legal Protection

As the #StaySecure campaign wrapped up, Aarushi and Sophia felt a renewed sense of purpose in their respective fields. What began as a harrowing experience for them and Kaneera ultimately led to personal growth, a deeper understanding of their strengths, and a realization of the real impact they could make. Together, they'd faced digital threats and emerged more empowered, determined to help others facing the often treacherous world of online security and legal rights.

The campaign's success sparked a cascade of new opportunities. Messages flooded in from individuals and organizations seeking advice, sharing personal stories, and asking for guidance. Inspired by the outpouring of support, Aarushi and Sophia knew that their journey was only beginning. Their experiences had ignited a fire within them-a desire to not only protect their loved ones but also pave the way for safer, more informed online communities.

Aarushi's Path: Becoming a Digital Security Advocate

Aarushi had always known she wanted to work in online security, but this experience had shown her the importance of extending that knowledge to others. She felt a newfound responsibility to share what she'd learned, to demystify online security, and to make protective measures accessible to everyone, especially young people who, like Kaneera, might be unaware of the lurking dangers.

Through the #StaySecure campaign, Aarushi realized that her passion for online security could go beyond simply detecting threats and protecting systems. She wanted to create a ripple effect, educating people on how to recognize and defend themselves against digital dangers in an approachable way. She began exploring ways to offer free workshops, tutorials, and online content geared toward different age groups and communities.

Working late one evening, she received an email from a nonprofit organization dedicated to digital literacy in underserved communities. They'd seen her campaign and wanted her to collaborate on a project that would teach online security basics in schools. This was the opportunity she'd been hoping for-a chance to bring her expertise to a broader audience and make online security an accessible concept.

She dove into the project with enthusiasm, designing courses and resources tailored for teenagers, young adults, and families. Her materials weren't packed with technical jargon; instead, she broke down complex ideas into digestible bits of information using real-life analogies and interactive activities. She wanted her students to feel empowered, not intimidated, by technology.

Aarushi also started a weekly blog and YouTube channel, where she shared tips, tricks, and cautionary tales drawn from her experiences. She covered topics ranging from password safety and phishing awareness to avoiding oversharing online. Each video and article felt like a personal conversation with her audience-one friend to another, looking out for each other in an increasingly connected world.

Her blog and channel quickly gained traction, and her following grew. Messages poured in thanking her for her approachable advice, and many shared their own stories of narrowly avoiding or surviving online scams. The support was overwhelming, and it reaffirmed Aarushi's belief that her knowledge could truly make a difference.

As her presence in the online security field expanded, Aarushi began to receive invitations to speak at conferences, particularly those focused on digital rights and security for young women. It was intimidating at first, but she embraced the opportunity, confident that her voice-and her story-could inspire others. In time, Aarushi's work grew into a community movement. People came to her for advice and practical help, and she proudly wore the role of a digital security advocate.

Sophia's Journey: Protecting Digital Rights through Law

For Sophia, the journey had taken her to a place where her passion for justice and her knowledge of online threats intersected perfectly. Her experiences have shown her firsthand the power that legal expertise could have in combating digital threats. She was determined to continue her studies in law with a focus on digital rights and online privacy, areas that she now felt deeply connected to.

Sophia knew that the legal landscape was constantly evolving to keep pace with new cyber threats. She wanted to help shape these policies, advocating for better protections and stronger consequences for those who used technology to harm others. With her characteristic determination, she sought opportunities to deepen her knowledge in digital law, signing up for specialized courses and networking with legal professionals who shared her vision.

An opportunity soon arose when she was invited to intern with a digital rights advocacy organization. They worked on cases involving privacy rights, online harassment, and data protection, and their mission was to ensure that individuals could feel safe in the digital realm. For Sophia, it was a dream come true. She immersed herself in the organization's work, assisting with cases and helping craft policies aimed at protecting online users.

As part of her internship, Sophia was tasked with researching international laws on cyber harassment and privacy. She was surprised by the gaps she found-many countries lacked comprehensive laws to address the new forms of abuse emerging online. She realized that legal systems had not fully caught up with the realities of the digital world, leaving victims with limited recourse in cases of cyberstalking, doxxing, and data theft.

Seeing this gap fueled her desire to make a difference on a larger scale. She began drafting a proposal for a new set of guidelines and legal protections tailored to the modern digital landscape, covering issues like identity theft, revenge pornography, and online harassment. Her goal was to present these guidelines to her organization, hoping they could use them as a framework to advocate for legislative change.

Sophia's passion and hard work didn't go unnoticed. Her supervisors encouraged her to take on more responsibility, giving her a platform to present her findings at workshops and community events. She became a voice for change, explaining the complexities of digital law in clear terms, encouraging people to report incidents, and offering advice on how to seek legal protection when needed.

Inspired by Aarushi's educational outreach, Sophia also started sharing resources online. She created a series of infographics and articles, simplifying legal rights and the steps people could take if they found themselves targeted by online threats. She wanted to make sure that everyone, regardless of their legal knowledge, could feel confident in standing up for themselves.

Through her advocacy, Sophia became known as a champion of digital rights, particularly for women and young people. She encouraged her followers to stay informed, reminding them that the law could be a powerful tool in defending their rights. She spoke openly about the challenges of pursuing justice in a rapidly changing online world, but she also emphasized that, together, they could push for meaningful reform.

A Shared Vision: Safeguarding the Future

Despite the different paths Aarushi and Sophia were taking, they both knew they would continue to support each other, working toward a shared vision of a safer digital world. They remained close friends and collaborators, often calling each other to discuss new developments, brainstorm ideas, or seek advice. Their bond had grown even stronger, forged through their journey and commitment to making a difference.

The success of the #StaySecure campaign had left a lasting impact on them both. They continued to see stories in the media about young people falling victim to digital threats, but they no longer felt helpless. They had become advocates, equipped not only with knowledge but with the conviction to educate others and push for change.

As they sat together in Aarushi's room one evening, discussing their future projects, Aarushi looked at Sophia with a smile. "You know, I never thought online security could be so... personal," she admitted. "I always saw it as this abstract thing, protecting networks and systems. But now, it feels like I'm protecting people-just like you do."

Sophia nodded. "I feel the same. Cyberlaw seemed so technical, but now, I see it's really about defending people's rights and freedoms. The law may take time to catch up, but that doesn't mean we can't make a difference now."

With a renewed sense of purpose, they made a pact to continue their work-Aarushi as an advocate for online security education and Sophia as a crusader for digital rights. They knew that their journey was just beginning and that there would be challenges ahead, but they were ready to face them together.

Their experience had transformed them, showing them that the digital world could be just as complex, risky, and in need of protection as the physical one. They weren't just protecting themselves anymore; they were paving the way for others to follow, empowering people to take control of their online lives, protect their privacy, and defend their rights.

As they said their goodbyes that night, each knew that their work was far from over. There were countless people out there who needed to hear their message and who needed guidance and support in navigating the digital world safely. And with each new step, they took Aarushi and Sophia were ready to meet that challenge, committed to making the internet a safer place for everyone.

www.ingramcontent.com/pod-product-compliance
Lightning Source LLC
LaVergne TN
LVHW052325200926
848481LV00002B/675
9781916865273